The Global Debt Crisis *AND*
How We Can Get Out of It

The Global Debt Crisis *AND* How We Can Get Out of It

JASON GOODWIN

OPEN BOOK
EDITIONS
A Jacob-Jordan Partner

iUniverse®

THE GLOBAL DEBT CRISIS AND HOW WE CAN GET OUT OF IT

Copyright © 2016 Jason Goodwin.
Author Credits: Andrew Featherstone

iUniverse books may be ordered through booksellers or by contacting:

iUniverse
1663 Liberty Drive
Bloomington, IN 47403
www.iuniverse.com
1-800-Authors (1-800-288-4677)

ISBN: 978-1-4917-9513-2 (sc)
ISBN: 978-1-4917-9514-9 (e)

Print information available on the last page.

iUniverse rev. date: 09/16/2016

CONTENTS

PART III

ACKNOWLEDGMENTS

I don't know if this book will succeed in its purpose, but if it does have something of value to offer, it will be because of the kind efforts of an Israeli man named Jerry Waxman. It's been more than ten years since I first met Jerry and asked him to edit this writing. If I can write, then it's thanks to Jerry.

Also thanks to Maggie and Mitchel of the Tellwell team out of Victoria, British Colombia. Publishers who gave a more recent edit of this book and valuable advice that is much appreciated by this fledgling author.

And special thanks to Ashley and Joseph at iUniverse. Ashley shared good creative input and wonderful advice, and she also inspired me to finish this book. I might not have accomplished that without her. Joseph sold me on the edit and more. Thanks, Joseph.

And much thanks to Chris D., who gave the final and best edit to date.

I would also like to acknowledge in advance the music of M83. When this book is made into a movie, I hope the songs "Outro" and "Wait" can be used in the soundtrack. For that matter, any songs by M83 are more than welcome. (Just kidding about the movie, but I couldn't resist).

For a little inspiration before starting this book, everyone is warmly encouraged to view the above-mentioned songs given below on YouTube. With amazing scenery and some of the most astonishing achievements of skill, courage, and cinematography you will ever see.

https://www.youtube.com/watch?v=fHfgtrHh0Ec
https://www.youtube.com/watch?v=YkbthU3W_AY
https://www.youtube.com/watch?v=x34FhtJ-L-0
https://www.youtube.com/watch?v=lAwYodrBr2Q

PART I

"*The world is governed by very different personages from what is imagined by those who are not behind the scenes.*"

—Benjamin Disraeli, first Prime Minister of England, 1844. Coningsby, The New Generation.

"*I care not what puppet is placed upon the throne of England to rule the Empire on which the sun never sets. The man that controls Britain's money supply controls the British Empire, and I control the British money supply.*"

—Baron Nathan Mayer de Rothschild, 1840-1915

"*The few who understand the system, will either be so interested from its profits or so dependent on its favors, that there will be no opposition from that class.*"

—Mayer Amschel Bauer Rothschild, 1744-1812

CHAPTER 1

The Global Debt Crisis

Greece is crippled by debt. Portugal, Ireland, Spain, Italy, Japan, China, and the United States all deeply troubled by debt—and so are many more nations. And too many families are hamstrung by debt.

Excessive debt seems to be a universal problem gripping the world. The Joint Chiefs of Staff have called America's national debt "the single biggest threat to national security."[1]

Consider the unrest in Syria, Iraq, Egypt, Ukraine, and so on. What do all these places and peoples have in common? Too many are struggling and jobless, which may be why they are so angry.

Their anger naturally stems from not having a legitimate channel to grow and fulfill their dreams in life, such as marrying, buying a home, and building a family. And then living life to the fullest in peace and security.

Many are missing valid ways to achieve their goals. In their frustration and torment, some choose to take up guns and join the Islamic State. And without jobs, they certainly have the time to do so.

So what is the root cause of the debt crisis and civil unrest that is slowly killing life? It's commonly understood that before a solution to a problem can be found, the underlying cause must first be located.

After a careful examination of the debt crisis and other related symptoms, this book endeavors to uncover the cause of the debt crisis, and thereby point a way to a solution that not only promises to reduce our taxes by 50 percent and more, but also lead us out of our debt crisis.

PART II

"We have come to be one of the worst ruled, one of the most completely controlled and dominated governments in the civilized world—no longer a government by free opinion, no longer a government by conviction and the vote of the majority, but a government by the opinion and the duress of small groups of dominant men."

— President Woodrow Wilson, A Call for The Emancipation of the Generous Energies of a People By New York And Garden City Doubleday, Page & Company 1913

*"A great industrial nation is controlled by its system of credit. Our system of credit is privately concentrated. The growth of the nation, therefore, and all our activities are in the hands of a few men who, even if their action be honest and intended for the public interest, are necessarily concentrated upon the great undertakings in which their own money is involved and who necessarily, by very reason of their own limitations, chill and check and destroy genuine economic freedom. **This is the greatest question of all, and to this statesman, must address themselves with an earnest determination to serve the long future and the true liberties of men.**"*

—President Woodrow Wilson, THE NEW FREEDOM, Section VIII: "Monopoly, Or Opportunity?", p. 185

CHAPTER 2

Our Market and Banking Systems

Banks are the exclusive first buyers of companies as they are sold during an *initial public offering* or IPO. Moreover, banks are permitted by governments to multiply money twenty times over when purchasing assets, such as companies.

For example, Apple Inc. went public in 1980 for $100 million. Assume for a moment that ten banks underwrote the Apple IPO. Each bank only requires half a million dollars to buy $10 million dollars' worth of Apple stock.

This is called the *money multiplier effect* of the *fractional reserve* banking system. It enables a bank to turn half a million dollars—into ten million dollars! Banks have two sources for the initial half million dollars to be multiplied: overnight lending with the central bank, and our money on deposit in their banks. More on these points in a moment.

Initially, the underwriting banks sell their newly purchased IPO companies to other banks, and often they sell to private banks. If a company looks to be very valuable, such as an oil company, then it would not be surprising for many of the selling banks to have the same principle owners as the buying banks.

Why transfer ownership from public to private banks?

Public banks are required to make public financial statements, such as earnings. Whereas, private banks can keep everything confidential. If the earnings of some private banks became public knowledge, it would be noticed.

Banks generally buy and sell directly with each other, rather than use a stock *exchange* on the *secondary market* (a.k.a. the *open* or *public market*). Furthermore, banks can do their buying and selling in something called *dark pools*, which as the name suggests, is a way of keeping it dark or hidden.

If each bank sells 5 percent of its Apple IPO holdings, this would generate enough money for each bank to repay the central bank what they borrowed to acquire Apple Inc. This would still leave these banks owning 95 percent of outstanding shares.

Note that for these banks to become the new principle owners of Apple Inc., it didn't cost these banks—or their owners—anything. That's because we paid for it. More on this point in a moment. As the new owners, these banks now receive most of the earnings, either as *dividend* payments or as *retained earnings.*

Dividends are company earnings paid to the owner stockholders. Earnings that are not paid as *dividends* to the owners, stays with the company to become *retained earnings;* this usually increases the company's stock value proportionately.

Money borrowed from the central bank is new government money. The Central bank is a part or aspect of our government (and if it's not—then it should be). New money made by our government (via our central bank) is a public asset that belongs to all of us. At the very least, it belongs to our government.

When banks purchase assets, they are using our money on deposit, or our money created new by our government. And since our money is used, we assume most of the risk, but somehow bankers receive all the reward. How can a few bankers be the new owners of all these companies, when they were all paid for by us—using our money?

Multiply the above many thousands of times, for the many thousands of companies that have gone public over the years. In the United States that's $25 trillion worth of public companies that have been purchased with our money—and yet somehow mostly owned by only a few financiers.

Over the past one hundred years (for North America, three hundred years for Europe), governments have expanded the money supply roughly a thousand times, by essentially just giving this new government money to bankers. Bankers will be quick to say that money borrowed from the central bank is a loan that must be returned with interest.

However, for every new dollar borrowed from the central bank, a bank can buy twenty dollars' worth of property. By selling one dollar of that property, they payback the dollar they borrowed, but this still leaves the banks holding nineteen dollars' worth of property—that never gets paid back!

There is another aspect to be aware of. There are *common shares,* and then there are *special* and *preferred shares*. There is a *special* class of share (*class B*) that has the same voting power as ten *common shares*. Likewise, *special* and *preferred shares* can have much higher dividend payouts than *common shares. Common shares* greatly outnumber *special* and *preferred shares*.

Therefore, it is possible for the general public to own 90 percent of a company (by number of shares) and yet most of the control and *dividend* payments belong to only a few *special* and *preferred shareholders*. Sometimes common shares have little or no dividends. In that case, what earnings are not paid out as *dividends* (to the *special* and *preferred shareholders)*, becomes *retained earnings*.

Special and *preferred* shares are seldom (if ever) sold on the *secondary market*—where you and I can buy in. Only *common shares* are sold on the *secondary* or *public market*. As the new owners, the banks decide what shares they will sell, at what price, and to whom.

Generally, hedge funds, mutual funds, and other institutional investors are the first to buy from banks. And for this they have their *road show*, where banks give presentations to *preferred customers* on upcoming IPO companies to be sold.

In another time, the *road show* was called the *dog and pony show*. The companies with risk were the dogs, and the companies with promise the ponies. Bankers tend to hold on to more of the ponies and sell the dogs.

Banks generally sell at least 10 percent of their company holdings, and often much more if a company looks to have some risk. Banks sell 5 percent in order to payback the initial amount they borrowed to buy the company, and then sell another 5 percent to satisfy capital requirements. This is explained in more detail in Addendum A.

After hundreds of years of this market, banking, and monetary system, some well-connected private bankers have amassed such a vast fortune that they are able to purchase promising companies even before they reach the IPO phase.

Private bankers also became *venture capitalists* and *angel investors*, fronting seed money to start-up companies; usually in exchange for half or more of the companies. It's not only public companies affected by this financial system. Many private companies have also been purchased with our money, yet they are mostly owned by only a few financiers.

Our financial system has been called a zero-sum game. For a few to be up billions of dollars—via the process described above—then the rest of us must be in debt tens of thousands of dollars. This debt often comes by way of government debt, at the federal, state, and municipal levels. Which many of us overlook, but it's mathematically inevitable, since everything must sum to zero.

Why must all accounts sum to zero?

Think of a game of poker. For some to be up, the rest must be down. If five people sit at the table, and each starts the game with one hundred dollars—and the game ends with one person having five hundred dollars—then the rest must have zero left.

With this analogy, each player starts the game with one hundred dollars. However, in life, we all start out with zero dollars. Unless our families or the lottery give us some wealth. But whatever amount they give us, theirs is also reduced by that same amount. Since really, we all start out with zero dollars, it all sums to zero. It is possible to explain this sum-to-zero result by considering only core principles of accounting.

How has our present banking system been so overlooked, by so many, for so long? Few study economics. Most people have little knowledge of our market, banking, and monetary systems. We all assumed that for these financial systems to have lasted in plain view for many hundreds of years, then it must be legal and lawful.

Slavery lasted in plain view for many thousands of years, and it was legal and lawful for all that time. It's only recently that people realized slavery is criminal. Just because our present banking system happens to be legal now, doesn't necessarily make it right. Someday we will look back on our present financial system and realize it was as criminal and cruel as slavery.

"People of the nation do not understand our banking and monetary system, for if they did, I believe there would be a revolution before tomorrow morning." [2]
—Henry Ford

"I see in the near future a crisis approaching that unnerves me and causes me to tremble for the safety of my country. As a result of the war, corporations have been enthroned, and an era of corruption in high places will follow, and the money power of the country will endeavor to prolong its reign, by working upon the prejudices of the people. Until all wealth is aggregated in the hands of a few, and the Republic is destroyed." [3]
— Abraham Lincoln

In that time, the word *republic* was synonymous with *democracy*. Lincoln meant that democracy would be destroyed. This has already happened. It's not democracy; it is legalized bribery. John Boehner proved this when he handed out millions in checks to members of Congress just minutes before a vote on whether or not to continue a billion-dollar subsidy to the tobacco industry.

The tobacco lobby was buying votes with those checks—kickback checks. Evil has no shame. Politicians cannot help themselves. I pity those who take bribe money because I know what waits for them in the end.

"I have two great enemies, the Southern army in front of me, and the bankers to my rear. Of the two, the one to my rear is my greatest foe." [4]

— Abraham Lincoln

Some armchair historians have speculated that bankers may have played a part in the assassination of President Lincoln. They like to cite the fact that Lincoln was the first and last president to fund government by printing money directly, rather than borrowing it from bankers.

Lincoln's money came to be known as *"greenbacks"* because the money was green and used to buy backs (people, labor). Lincoln had to print the money to fund the war. Bankers would not lend money to support the North. The bankers did not want to see an end to slavery. You might even say that slavery was their stock-in-trade; in a way, we are still slaves to debt.

Interested readers and policy makers may refer to addendums A, B, and C at the end of this book for a more in-depth clarification of the world's banking and monetary system, which is based on the European archetype.

"The Bankers own the Earth. Take it away from them, but leave them the power to create deposits, and with the flick of a pen they will create enough deposits to buy it back again.

However, take it away from them [the power to make money("deposits")], *and all the fortunes like mine will disappear, and they ought to disappear, for this world would be a happier and better world to live in.*

But if you wish to remain slaves of the Bankers and pay for the cost of your own slavery, let them continue to create deposits."

—Sir Josiah Stamp, President of the Bank of England (1920s)

Source: Silas Walter Adams (1958). The legalized crime of banking and a constitutional remedy. Boston: Meador. Pp 58

"The hand that gives is above the hand that takes. Money has no motherland, financiers are without patriotism and without decency; their sole object is gain"

—Napoleon Bonaparte

"Most Americans have no real understanding of the operation of the international moneylenders. ... The accounts of the Federal Reserve System have never been audited. It operates outside the control of Congress and ... manipulates the credit of the United States"

—*Senator Barry Goldwater (R-AZ)*

"This [Federal Reserve Act] *establishes the most gigantic trust* [business entity] *on earth. When the President* [Wilson] *signs this bill, the invisible government of the monetary power will be legalized.... the worst legislative crime of the ages is perpetrated by this banking and currency bill."*

—Charles A. Lindbergh, Sr., December 23, 1913. Congressional records.

CHAPTER 3

Technology and Employment

Tractors on farms, robots in factories, heavy equipment in construction, forestry, and mining. Along with computers in science, engineering, and business—have all provided for a general 50 percent reduction in the amount of human labor needed to deliver the same level of production and the same standard of living.

This has the potential to cause a massive 50 percent layoff and force governments to tax, borrow, and spend to make jobs, but they are often unproductive jobs.

If all goods and services cost half as much to produce, producers could opt to pass this 50 percent cost savings on to consumers as a general 50 percent price reduction, while keeping profits the same.

With everything costing half as much, everyone only needs to work half as much to maintain the same standard of living as before. Everyone would keep their jobs, but work only half as many hours, avoiding a massive 50 percent layoff, crushing debt, and excessive taxation.

However, what if producers rather than keeping profits the same by passing cost savings on to consumers as lower prices, instead opt to double their profits, by keeping prices the same? Even while their costs have been cut in half by new technology.

In such a scenario, everyone would need to continue to work the same amount as before, because the cost of living would not have changed. However, because of new technology, now only half the labor is needed.

This scenario creates a massive 50 percent layoff that corresponds to the 50 percent savings in labor brought about by new technology. Ever since the Second World War, the approach of governments has been to tax, borrow, and spend to create jobs, along with welfare.

"The fantastic tricks which financiers play–and which they cover up with high technical terms. The people are on the side of sound money. They are so unalterably on the side of sound money that it is a serious question how they would regard the system under which they live, if they once knew what the initiate [bankers] can do with it."

—Henry Ford, My life and Work, Pg. 179

"The problem isn't that Bernie Sanders is a crazy-pants cuckoo bird. It's that we've all become so accustomed to stage-managed, focus-group-driven candidates that authenticity comes across as lunacy."

—Jon Stewart

"If we can find the money to kill people, we can find the money to help people."

—Tony Benn.

"Many people consider the things government does for them to be social progress, but they regard the things government does for others to be socialism."

—Earl Warren

CHAPTER 4

The Big If

But what if everyone was an equal owner of most corporations? Then, even if producers respond to the labor-saving cost-reducing efficiencies of new technologies, by keeping product prices the same, and thereby doubling profits—the doubled profits would then be dispersed to everyone equally.

This would have the effect of matching each person's income from work, with an equal amount of new income from dividends, thereby effectively doubling each person's income.

Half-time work then provides the same amount of income as full-time work did before. Hence, everyone only needs to work half as many hours, and there would be no layoffs, debt, or taxes [10]. The two paths lead to the same end result.

One path lowers the cost of living by half, while incomes stay the same. The other path doubles incomes, while the cost of living stays the same. With either path, we all stay on the job, but only work half as many hours, while continuing to enjoy the same standard of living usually associated with full-time work. And the promise of robots, automation, and technology is realized.

Governments were made for people and not the other way around. Our government belongs to us—the people—and not we to our government. Ergo, new money created by our government, via our central bank, really belongs to all of us, and not only to a few bankers.

This misplaced asset ownership, specifically refers to corporations that have *gone public,* or have been financed by money derived from the present banking system. There are many large corporations that started as a small family business, and with courage, wit, and hard work, they grew to become massive multinational conglomerates. Usually, this was done by taking on more partners along the way.

They are the rightful owners of their companies—job creators who have earned their place as the most capable among us in the market place. Problems arise when company founders sell their companies in an IPO process involving banks in combination with the present market system.

Bankers then believe themselves to be the rightful new owners of these companies when they are not—we are! It was our money that bankers used to buy company assets. Specifically, our money on deposit was used, and our money made new by our government was used.

Moreover, there are many nonpublic companies that have also received financing from banks in exchange for substantial ownership. They were financed directly with bank money (our money), or indirectly with money descending from banks and not money earned.

As it turns out, we are all equal and majority owners

of most large corporations, and that's the way it has always been. Somehow, as a group, we don't realize this yet. Just as for many thousands of years, countless billions were sold into a lifetime of slavery, torture, and torment. Really, they were always free, but we needed time to realize it. With hope, now it's time for the next level of awakening.

Some people may call the ideas of this book "socialism", and point to places like Russia and Cuba and say, "See? Socialism doesn't work." First of all, those places are not examples of socialism—and they never were. They are, however, examples of clever rebranding.

Norway is an example of socialism, and per capita, it is the wealthiest nation on earth. Norway is well over a trillion dollars up—and for only 5 million people. Contrast that with the United States: $22 trillion down, when state and municipal debt is included, and zero sovereign wealth fund.

However, if the United States had put a trade embargo on Norway, as it did on Cuba, Russia, and other nations, then even with all its oil, Norway would be just as destitute as Cuba. And some analysts would point to Norway and say, "See? Socialism doesn't work." They would be overlooking sixty years of economic sanctions.

Cuba, Russia, Iran, and many other nations have been attacked economically with economic sanctions and trade embargos. If Cuba had failed on its own, without so much external interference, then we could have said now, "Whatever that was, it's not working." But who knows? Maybe Cuba and Russia would have done just fine, were it not for external competing factors interfering.

A very long time ago, Russia started out in a socialist

direction. Groups of people collectively owned farmland and shared the work and earnings. They were called communes, which is where *communism* comes from.

In that sense, a commune is the same as a kibbutz in Israel, but we don't see Americans calling Israelis "commies" or "kibbutzies" and subjecting Israel to a trade embargo for sixty years.

Russia under Stalin murdered millions of its own people, so we can safely say for sure that Russia was not socialist. It was an extreme example of "anti-socialism." Russia is a very different nation now, but it is still not socialist per se.

Russia and Cuba are examples of *command economies* where the central government plays an overriding role. It is interesting to note that the United States has also resorted to a command economy a few times in its history, and could not have survived the Civil War or World War II without it. Moreover, they were the most industrially productive times in American history.

During the Great Recession of 2008, the United States would have collapsed, just like it did in the Great Depression. The only thing that saved the United States from the abyss was its shameful ability to counterfeit money to pay its bills and buy goods abroad.

The United States may not be able to make cars and phones competitively, but we can still make money (literally) and export it globally through the World Bank and IMF. Many times the United States would have failed bigger than Russia or Cuba, but unlike them, we did it on our own—without any outside interference. And unlike them, we were able to counterfeit our way out—not earn our way out—like they did.

America's lack of a trade surplus is not from any lack of talent or ability; it is only because the American dollar is so strong. As a producer, the United States has priced itself out of the consumer-goods market, but partly makes up for this by being a major producer and exporter of high-end high-tech products. However, it is not enough to produce a net trade surplus. The United States has not shown a trade surplus in more than 40 years.

The United States does not need to have a trade surplus to have more dollars (wealth). The United States can just print more dollars as it likes. Costa Rica can also do quantitative easing and print more Costa Rican pesos, but its money is only good in Costa Rica. American dollars are good everywhere. For a continuation and clarification of this discussion, see addendum E: The Wealth of Nations.

"The real truth of the matter is, as you and I know, that a financial element in the larger centers has owned the Government ever since the days of Andrew Jackson."

—Franklin D. Roosevelt,
In a letter written to Colonel Edward Mandell House, 21 November 1933.
Source: F.D.R.: His Personal Letters, edited by Elliott Roosevelt
New York: Duell, Sloan and Pearce, 1950, pg. 373.

"Until the control of the issue of currency and credit is restored to government and recognized as its most conspicuous and sacred responsibility, all talks of the sovereignty of Parliament and of democracy is idle and futile. Once a nation parts with the control of its credit, it matters not who makes the laws"

—William Mackenzie King, Prime Minister of Canada. 1934.

"Vast accession of strength from their younger recruits, who having nothing in them of the feelings or principles of '76 [year of the declaration of independence] *now look to a single and splendid government of an Aristocracy, founded on banking institutions and monied in corporations, under the guise and cloak of their favored branches of manufactures, commerce, and navigation, riding and ruling over the plundered ploughman and beggared yeomanry."*

[Yeomanry refers to a small military unit comprised of Yeomen. Yeomen are people who usually work in the fields as farmers.]

— Thomas Jefferson, in a letter to William Branch Giles.

One year before Jefferson's death and fifty years since his declaration of independence.

CHAPTER 5

A Little Historical Perspective

With the advent of technology, tractors replaced oxen and farmers, robots replaced factory workers. Machines and power tools replaced miners and other laborers. Along with computers that displaced engineers, scientists, accountants, architects, artists, and so on.

Increased unemployment tends to depress wages as more people compete for fewer positions (supply and demand of labor). With lower wages, those still employed have less money to spend. This reduces consumption, and with time, further reduces production, thereby generating more layoffs.

Each cycle feeds into the next. One such cycle caused the Great Depression. Today, we have minimum wage laws that put a lower limit on how far this cycle can depress wages and effectively disrupt it. However, if living costs go up faster than wages, then it's just the same as *real wages* going lower. If wages stay set, but over time living costs double, then it's just the same as *real wages* went down by half.

Additionally, now we have a global economy. Other

nations, such as China, may not have minimum wage laws, but even if they do, their minimum wage might be only a dollar a day. In a global economy, this circumvents our own wage laws and safeguards.

The Second World War put an end to the Great Depression, by essentially putting everyone back to work. This gave birth to the *tax, borrow, and spend* approach, which has become the mainstay for governments to stimulate their economies and create jobs. As this approach became ever more costly, some governments have also added a subsistence approach with welfare.

Technology continues to advance, and the potential for unemployment continues to grow. Governments have increased their spending to go ever deeper into debt. So that now we have a debt crisis gripping much of the world. And most nations have yet to show that they can even start to pay down their debt or even balance their budgets. They keep deficit spending and increasing debt to stimulate their economies and create jobs.

This might seem to suggest that technology is the root cause of underemployment, crushing debt, and excessive taxation. But this only means that we have not yet implemented the correct solution. Borrow, tax, and spend is not a solution; it is part of the problem.

As we look deeper, we find the true source of underemployment, crushing debt, and excessive taxation—is not technology—it is artificial obstacles. Before examining the obstacles, we lead in with a little primer about free-market dynamics.

"The money powers prey upon the nation in times of peace and conspire against it in times of adversity. The banking powers are more despotic than a monarchy, more insolent than autocracy, more selfish than bureaucracy. They denounce as public enemies all who question their methods or throw light upon their crimes."

—Abraham Lincoln, in a letter to Col. William F. Elkins, Nov. 21, 1864,

Archer H. Shaw, The Lincoln Encyclopedia (New York: Macmillan, 1950), p. 40

"Bank-paper must be suppressed, and the circulating medium must be restored to the nation to whom it belongs."

—Thomas Jefferson to John Wayles Eppes, Monticello, 24 June 1813.

"The world will not be destroyed by those who do evil, but by those who watch them without doing anything"

—Albert Einstein

"Experience declares that man is the only animal which devours his own kind, for I can apply no milder term to the governments of Europe, and to the general prey of the rich on the poor."

— Tomas Jefferson in a letter to Edward Carrington, 16 January 1787

CHAPTER 6

Free-Market Dynamics Primer

Suppose a new study reveals that oranges prevent illness, and keeps you fit, young, and energetic. This good news could cause a run on oranges, and initially result in a shortage of oranges. According to the principle of supply and demand, the increased demand for oranges, but initial lack of supply—would cause the price of oranges to increase sharply.

The greater demand and profits of orange production would attract more producers to the orange market. In time, this would increase the supply of oranges to satisfy the demand. Eventually, the price for oranges would come down again, so that everyone could enjoy the lifesaving value of oranges.

This is an example of free-market dynamics at work. In a truly free economy, the balancing of prices with supply and demand is completely automatic, and no government intervention is needed. In a balanced free economy, the state of least effort for greatest gain happens naturally and effortlessly.

However, what if the orange producers were able to

make it difficult for others to enter the orange market? They could keep the price of oranges high, by keeping the supply low, and the orange producers could continue to take a disproportionate profit.

Labor is needed where there is a shortage of labor. When one area experiences a shortage of labor—and high earnings as a result—the high earnings are meant to serve a purpose. The purpose is to attract more people to work in that area. When artificial obstacles prevent more people from working in some area, the natural dynamics of a free economy are compromised. This creates an economic imbalance.

Artificial obstacles come in a variety of forms and circumstances.

"By a continuing process of inflation, governments can confiscate, secretly and unobserved, an important part of the wealth of their citizens ... in a manner which not one man in a million can diagnose"

—John Maynard Keynes

"When plunder becomes a way of life for a group of men living together in society, they create for themselves in the course of time, a legal system that authorizes it, and a moral code that glorifies it."

—Economic Sophisms, Frederic Bastiat 1801-1850

They know that America is not a place of which it can be said, as it used to be, that a man may choose his own calling and pursue it just as far as his abilities enable him to pursue it; because to-day, if he enters certain fields, there are organizations which will use means against him that will prevent his building up a business which they do not want to have built up; organizations that will see to it that the ground is cut from under him and the markets shut against him. For if he begins to sell to certain retail dealers, to any retail dealers, the monopoly will refuse to sell to those dealers, and those dealers, afraid, will not buy the new man's wares."

—President Woodrow Wilson, The New Freedom, Chapter I: The Old Order Changeth

CHAPTER 7

The Obstacles

The first and most damaging obstacles are in education. The second most damaging obstacles are in the area of our market, banking, and monetary systems.

The Certification Obstacle

It is common sense and common practice for experts in a field to train others who want to enter their field. Hence, only doctors are qualified to train and certify new doctors. Only engineers are qualified to train and certify new engineers. The same is true in many other professions.

While this makes sense from the standpoint of training and qualifications, it also creates a conflict of interest. When members of a profession choose whom and how many to train and certify as new members of their profession, they can raise the value of their services by keeping membership small.

Take for example the field of orthodontics; only about 2 percent of dentists who apply are admitted. Why is it only 2 percent? Orthodontists say that it's because orthodontics is a very difficult and exact science.

But when you think about it, dentists drill into teeth, cut into gums, and perform surgery, but only 2 percent have the ability to put a little bend in a wire, and charge three hundred dollars for a minute or two of wire bending.

Perhaps, it is not only a matter of skills that makes orthodontics such a specialized field. As in other fields, perhaps there are factors unrelated to skills that make orthodontists an exclusive group.

By being such a small group in fairly high demand, orthodontists are able to charge exorbitant fees and earn much more than other dentists. While orthodontists enjoy the benefits of their specialty, it is unfortunate for those who need, and have needed this type of treatment, but are unable to afford the prohibitive fees.

Note: I wrote this section roughly twenty years ago. Things may have changed since then. Or perhaps they are the same. I leave this example here because there may be other nations where similar obstacles still exist. Canada may be one of them, but this book is not just about Canada, and not just for now, but also for our shared future.

The Money Obstacle

As companies go public, obstacles block us from having equal access to new government money via lending with the central bank. These obstacles stop us from multiplying that new government money twenty times over, and effectively keep us from creating our own new money in the process. And they block us from being among the first to use new government money and new bank-made money to buy IPO companies as they are sold.

However, bankers were not hindered by any of these obstacles. Why? The answer lies within the money obstacle. To acquire a banking license, some governments require startup capital in excess of a billion dollars—making money the obstacle to entry.

A banking license gives unlimited access to new government money via central bank lending. A license allows bank owners to multiply that new government money twenty times over—thereby effectively creating their own bank-made money in the process. And further permits bankers to be the first to buy companies, as they are sold during an initial public offering or IPO.

Other places, such as the Cayman Islands and Dubai, don't require as much startup capital for a banking license. They have total banking secrecy laws, numbered accounts (no names), and zero capital gains tax.

The Tariff Obstacle

In some developing regions, when farmers take their crops to market, they are stopped on the road by men holding AK-47 assault rifles. To continue on their way to market, the farmers must pay these armed men. This, of course, is robbery or extortion.

Goods such as chocolate and coffee go on to the United States and Europe where again they are stopped by men with guns. The importers of these goods must pay an import tariff before being allowed to continue on their way.

Note that import tariffs, as an obstacle to entry, cause goods to cost more. This is a common effect of all obstacles to pass. They impose extra costs and cause prices to rise. An obstacle to entry, such as an import tariff, can be defined as paying for permission to continue on our way—which is extortion or robbery.

The Permit Obstacle

Suppose you're about to purchase a quarter-acre housing lot selling for $50,000, but then you look across the road to see one hundred acres of farmland selling for only $2 million. You put a notice online that reads, "Looking for 100 people with $20,000 each, to collectively purchase 100 acres of farm land. That's one acre each at the very low cost of $20,000 per acre—as compared to $200,000 per acre."

So what's there to stop us from doing this?

If we try this, one quickly discovers that the hundred-acre parcel of land across the road is zoned for agriculture, even though it may not have been a working farm for many years. In Canada (and perhaps elsewhere), it is almost impossible for the average person to change this zoning from farming to residential.

Only certain developers have the needed connections in government to acquire the necessary permits and zoning in a reasonable time frame. This reduces the natural availability of land, thereby making land artificially much more expensive.

City administrators like to hide behind the rationalization that if they allow anyone to easily change land zoning, then this would cause urban sprawl. However, there would be no more homes than we have now—and no urban sprawl. All it would do is take away the undue profits that the present system gives to those with the necessary connections in government to get land zoned.

If everyone were free to zone land easily, the person selling land for $50,000 per quarter-acre lot would have to sell for much less. His land would still be built on first—but at the same price as the farmland.

Otherwise, people would just buy the farmland and build there instead. Developers would have to lower their prices to match that of the farmland, or there would be nothing artificial to stop people from building someplace else.

The Quota and License Obstacles

Suppose you work as a fisherman on the west coast of Canada to earn about $60,000 per year. One day you and the other fishermen working on the boat do the math and realize that you could double your earnings if you went into business for yourselves.

So what's there to stop us?

In Canada, one man owns most of the west coast commercial fishing quota, and the rest is owned by only a few more. And many quota holders are not even working fishermen, but they have the power to stop working fishermen from doing their jobs unless they are paid. This is extortion.

With import tariffs, it is easy to see how an extortion fee is required before being allowed to continue on our way. However, with fishing quotas, the extortion payment is not so obvious. Fishermen do not openly pay a fee to a quota holder.

If fishermen were not blocked from going into business for themselves (blocked by not having a quota), they could earn more by forming a partnership with the other fishermen working on the boat, sharing the catch, and making their own business.

The difference in earnings between what fishermen earn from working for someone else (with a quota) and what they would earn by working for themselves (with a quota), this difference in earnings is the hidden fee that fishermen pay to quota holders for their permission to continue with their jobs.

Quotas, permits, and licenses should not be distributed by auction or selling because then money becomes the barrier to entry. A fishing quota should be granted freely and equally among all the working fishermen, and there should be nothing to stop new fishermen from entering this line of work (if attracted by higher wages).

Note: I wrote this section roughly twenty years ago. Shortly after that I sent e-mails to the Department of Fisheries and Oceans, British Columbia. I conveyed my views on how fishing quotas should be handled.

They may have listened—or maybe not. I didn't bother to check on this now because even if they listened back then and changed the quota scheme, other nations may still have quotas, permits, and licenses structured with extortion.

This book is not just about fishing, or about Canada. And it's not only for now, but also for our shared future. I could have used taxi licensing for this discussion; both are structured in very similar ways. However, since the arrival of Uber, taxi licensing has started to change for the better in some regions.

Obstacles to Natural Resources

Mine owners represent an obstacle to entry. Everyone but the mine owners are restricted from entering and working a mine for personal gain. Owners do allow workers to enter and work their mines, but only on the condition that most of the miners' earnings are turned over to the mine owners.

Therefore, the effects of mine ownership are the same as with other obstacles to entry; the highest profits are realized by those who produce the least, while the cost of keeping a few owners rich is paid for by all consumers.

By definition, *natural resources* are part of nature, not man-made, and therefore belong to us all. The system proposed by this book (and discussed in detail in part 3), remedies obstacles to natural resources by making all miners the owners of their mines, by making you and everyone the owners of all companies. Why not? You paid for them after all.

Obstacles and Prices versus Labor

Envision a truly free economy without artificial obstacles. If 10 percent of the working population labors to produce cars, and if all cars produced are for domestic consumption, and we do not import any cars, then cars would represent 10 percent of the average person's life expense.

If car production requires half the workforce, then cars would cost half of the average person's life expense. In a free economy, the amount of labor that goes into producing something is naturally reflected by its cost/price.

A producer could try to charge more than the cost of production, but if overpricing persists, in a free economy there is nothing to block others (attracted by higher earnings) from entering the market.

This increases production and with it supply, which would bring prices down to a level even lower than before. In a free economy, we only pay for the cost of production, and not for the cost of permissions to continue on our way.

A free economy leads to a state of equilibrium and homeostasis. All of a nation's labor is then fully utilized (no unemployment) and with just the correct amount of labor in each area for optimum economic efficiency. Moreover, no labor is wasted on unproductive and counterproductive jobs. This creates a state of maximum production (gain) for least effort.

However, if cars cost 20 percent of average incomes, but the car industry employs only 2 percent of the labor force, then this means there are substantial extortion expenses from various obstacles on many levels.

The most significant and damaging of these obstacles, are the ones that put most of the ownership and earnings, of most large companies, in the hands of only a few. Specifically, the obstacles in our market, banking, and monetary systems as companies are sold in an IPO process.

If 10 percent of the population works to produce garments, and half of the garments produced stay for domestic consumption, while the other half are exported, and we do not import any garments, then in a free economy, garments would represent 5 percent of the average person's life expense.

Now suppose the government decides to give garment quotas, permits, or licenses to just a few individuals, say the factory owners. Now the garment workers would need to pay a fee to a quota holder for their permission to continue making garments.

As with fishing quotas, garment workers do not openly pay a fee to a quota holder. The difference in income, between what garment workers earn from working for someone else (with a quota), and what they would earn by working for themselves (with a quota), is the hidden fee that garment workers pay to a quota holder.

This expense is passed on to consumers and increases the cost of garments, which causes fewer garments to be purchased. This causes layoffs in the garment industry. The true source of underemployment, crushing debt, and excessive taxation is not technology. Artificial obstacles hinder how the economy as a whole adapts to new technology.

Before garment quotas, if the owner shareholders did not share profits fairly with workers, then there was nothing artificial to block garment workers from just going off and starting their own business.

However, with quotas this becomes impossible, and they are forced to work for whomever owns or controls the quotas—no matter how low the wages may get. It is the same with fishermen working together on the same boat, they cannot just go make their own business—not unless they have a fishing quota. They are forced to work for whomever owns or controls a quota. If they want to work as fishermen, then they will need to pay a quota holder for their permission—and that doesn't come cheap.

Note: Garment quotas are not currently active in Canada. However, I have lived in other nations that have or did have such garment quotas. Again, this book is not just for Canada, and not just for now, but also for our shared future.

Roughly twenty years ago, I was in a garment factory in a nation bordering China. A man and a woman pranced into the conference room and cheerfully said, "So, you have a quota?"

There had been some miscommunication at the security gate when I was let into the factory. I looked at them and said, "What do you mean by a quota?"

Without another word, they left as quickly as they had entered. A few minutes later, armed men escorted me out.

A few days before this factory meeting, I had discovered name-brand trousers selling for only three dollars apiece. It gave me an idea to buy thousands of garments and ship them to America and make a hefty profit.

A few days after that factory meeting I was in a bank; when, I met an American standing in a queue next to me. We talked for a long while. Every six months, he would fly into town to visit dozens of garment factories.

Garment factories had to pay him millions every year just for his signature on certain import documents.

Without his or some other quota holder's signature, the garments could not be shipped to the United States. He happened to mention that his father was a United States congressman, which may have had something to do with how he was able to get a garment import quota.

By now, the United States may have phased out such import quotas or perhaps not. I hear they come and go and then come again. I mention this here only as yet another example of how these quota-extortion schemes take shape.

However, that's not to say that quotas don't serve a purpose. If fish stocks are low, then fishing needs to be curtailed to prevent overfishing and protect fish stocks. There is a need for some quotas, but the correct and fair way is to reduce the amount that each fisherman can catch. Each fisherman should get an equal share of the quota. As fishermen come and go (depending on earnings) everyone in the area shares the quota.

If the quota goes too low from overfishing, then some fishermen will leave to greener pastures—if there are no fences (obstacles) around those greener pastures. Again, this book is not just about fishing. We could have used taxi licensing for this discussion, both are structured in similar ways.

Twenty years ago, I checked with American customs about importing garments without a quota holder's signature. It would have cost me over a hundred thousand dollars, which stopped me from doing this business.

Canada did not have import quotas to stop me, but had other ways to block us from doing this business. Garments could not be imported without a label or trademark, such as Dockers or Levi's. However, if we import garments with company labels, but do not have writs from those companies authorizing us as valid importers, customs will not permit those goods to pass, and we could even be sued by those companies.

If it had been possible to import garments without signatures, then we could have hired garment workers to work from their homes instead of a factory.

If we didn't have to pay millions for import signatures, then we could have paid workers much more to work from their homes. And if we didn't pay workers a fair wage, there would be nothing to stop them—or anyone—from just doing it themselves.

Sadly, such blocks are prevalent. Why? Because of all the Boehners in government. Because we elected those Boehners. Because we cannot see the forest for the trees or the good from the Boehners.

A year before the garment stuff in China, I was strolling along a beach in Victoria, BC. I started talking with a man on the beach. He was a commercial fisherman. I asked him how much fish they usually caught, what the market value typically was, how many men worked on the boat, the cost of the boat, and so on.

We ran the numbers together and I asked why they just didn't go into business for themselves and double their incomes. He was the first person to introduce me to the world of fishing quotas. He even told me the name of the man who owned 90 percent of the west coast commercial fishing quota. I confirmed everything he said with the Department of Fisheries and Oceans, BC.

The fishing and garment quotas got me started on this book.

Obstacles, Migration, and Employment

If a million people snuck across the border to find jobs, would it take away jobs from us? Because we live in a world with layer upon layer of artificial obstacles, the short answer is yes. However, in a world without obstacles, the answer would be no. In a truly free economy, it would not take away even one job from anyone.

We earn money to spend money. By spending our earnings, we generate jobs for others in the making of the things we buy. If someone works two jobs because he wants a house twice as big, does this take away a job from someone else? If twice the labor is needed to make a house twice as big, then perhaps not.

If we work Y hours to earn X dollars, but then in spending X dollars, Y hours of work are in turn generated for others, then no unemployment is generated for others—even if we choose to work two jobs or change our work area. However, there must be no artificial obstacles for this to hold true.

We work about thirty years to pay for our homes, but in that time, we only generate about one year of actual work time for those who build our homes. In a free economy, we would only have to work one year to pay for our homes. It only takes one man-year of labor to build them. Artificial obstacles cause this disparity. They greatly inflate the cost of land, lumber, labor, and money (borrowing).

Homes (in Canada) should only cost about $60,000 (one year's average wage). Presently, the average home price in Canada is roughly $400,000, but then it's not just $400,000, but well over a million dollars by the time interest charges are factored in.

Just think of it, we pay roughly a million dollars for something that you and your brother can build in only six months. How many years on the job would it take for you to save up a million dollars? Much more than one year— more like 30 years. And if done right land would be practically free[12].

Keep in mind that the people building our homes are also paying off their own million-dollar mortgages after interest charges. This expense has to be passed on to us as much higher fees for their services. However, if their own homes also only cost $60,000, then this savings can be passed on to us as much lower fees for their services. Thereby greatly lowering the cost of all homes for everyone.

Artificial obstacles breakdown the otherwise natural correlation between the amount of time we spend working, and the amount of work time we generate for others as we spend our earnings. Obstacles make unemployment, debt, and taxes, inevitable. A free economy makes unemployment optional, and debt and taxes much less.

In the preceding example, we used homes to explain the breakdown in correlation between the cost of a home, and the amount of labor generated from building a home. Most of the money spent on home building does **not** go to the people doing the actual work of home building.

Most of the money goes to the lenders, developers, and producers.

And "lenders, developers, and producers" really just means all the various companies that produce goods and services (and banks). And company earnings go to the owner stockholders. How much employment the owner stockholders generate in turn—as they spend their earnings—depends on how they spend their earnings.

If the owner stockholders spend their earnings on more land, then this does nothing to generate jobs, but only compounds the problem by pushing up land prices without also pushing up average incomes. If the owner stockholders spend on more cars, boats, or other items that require labor to produce them, then this does generate jobs, but not in proportion to the amount of money put in.

Why not in proportion to the amount of money put in?

When the average person spends, only a fraction of this spending reaches the people doing the actual work of producing. Most of the money goes to the owner stockholders (often financiers). The same dynamic happens when the owner stockholders spend their earnings. Most of their spending just boomerangs back to them.

If the owner financiers spend on more stocks or bonds, then again no jobs are generated from this kind of spending. Again, it only compounds the problem by pushing up prices across the board without also pushing up average incomes.

Money spent on stocks and bonds only goes to the previous owners of the stocks and bonds, and not to the companies that issued them. The same can be said of real-estate and commodity speculation.

If the owner financiers spend on newly issued stocks or bonds, purchased directly from the issuing company, then this kind of spending does reach the company to fund operations and generate jobs. But again, not in proportion to the amount of money put in. Most of the money just boomerangs back to the owner financiers. Besides, the only way to buy newly issued stocks or bonds is to be one of the underwriting banks during a stock or bond issuance.

This boomerang effect causes money to accumulate with the owner financiers, but at everyone else's expense. Financiers act like money sinks—sucking all the money out of the economy—and money is the lifeblood of the economy.

There is one more scenario to consider.

What if a segment of the population goes through a period of saving time, to spend later on some big ticket items, such as a home or a car? Prolonged saving time by enough people can cause unemployment, but often while some people are in saving mode, others have finished their saving time and are now in spending mode.

If there are enough people in the local economy, and there has not been any major war or genocide (to cause a generation gap), then usually peoples saving time is roughly balanced out by other people's spending time.

"These international bankers and Rockefeller-Standard Oil interests control the majority of the newspapers, and the columns in those papers, to club into submission, or drive out of office, officials who refuse to do the bidding of the powerful corrupt cliques which compose the invisible government."

— Theodore Roosevelt as reported in the New York Times, March 27th, 1918

"Here is what income and wealth inequality is about. Last year, the top 25 hedge fund managers made more than 24 billion, enough to pay the salaries of 425,000 public school teachers. This level of inequality is neither moral or sustainable."

—Sen Bernie Sanders (I-VT)

PART III

CHAPTER 8

A New Labor-Distribution Technology

Now that we have carefully delineated the root problem—artificial obstacles—the task of defining a solution now begins. Naturally, the obvious first step is to remove artificial obstacles in all their various forms.

With time, this alone may be enough to normalize and balance the economy. Nonetheless, we now introduce a system that is specifically designed to facilitate a transition to balance in the absence of artificial obstacles.

Under the proposed system, if we lost a job, we would continue to receive the same salary until we found new employment. However, to receive this salary, we would be required to study full-time until new employment was found. This combines with changes to postsecondary education.

Rather than studying many courses at one time, we study only one or two courses at a time. One course for half-time study (mornings or afternoons), and two courses for full-time study (mornings *and* afternoons).

Courses can be taught in short blocks—perhaps one-month blocks—with an exam at the end of each block.

Each block is repeated monthly, immediately following the end of each block. In that way, if we fail a block, we do not need to wait a year to retake the course. Rather, we can retake the block immediately, since all courses are repeated monthly.

Every course of study is open to anyone, provided we have completed the necessary prerequisite blocks. Every field of study would have an entry point or first block open to anyone. If we complete a block, then we are admitted into the next block, and so on without restriction.

With 2 percent unemployment, all those employed pay a 2 percent tax to his or her income to fully fund this system. The money from this tax is transferred as a salary to all those not employed and studying full-time. This tax puts enough money into the system to allow full-time students to continue receiving the same salary as when they were working.

With 4 percent unemployment, a 4 percent tax can fully fund this system and so on. With this system, it can be shown that most people will be working only half-time, while continuing to receive a full-time income. Study would be full-time, with substantial costs attached.

It is expected that people would favor more useable income from half-time employment, than less useable income from fulltime study, and would only use paid study as a means to upgrade in their current field, or to retrain for a new field.

People working half-time would always have the option of half-time study while working. We could opt to work mornings, while studying afternoons or vice versa. All courses are offered both mornings and afternoons. It is recommended that half-time study while working be priced at cost or perhaps even below cost.

Some of the cost of part-time study can be passed on to the full-time students. This would make part-time study while working cost less, and paid full-time study cost more. This would give further incentive for people to do their studying while working, and not just stop their jobs in order to receive paid full-time study.

This labor distribution system combines with the resource-management database.

"I am convinced there is only one way to eliminate these grave evils, namely through the establishment of a socialist economy, accompanied by an educational system which would be oriented toward social goals. In such an economy, the means of production are owned by society itself and are utilized in a planned fashion.

A planned economy, which adjusts production to the needs of the community, would distribute the work to be done among all those able to work and would guarantee a livelihood to every man, woman, and child.

The education of the individual, in addition to promoting his own innate abilities, would attempt to develop in him a sense of responsibility for his fellow men in place of the glorification of power and success in our present society."

—Albert Einstein

"There is no provision that all those able and willing to work will always be in a position to find employment. An army of unemployed almost always exists. The worker is constantly in fear of losing his job. Since unemployed and poorly paid workers do not provide a profitable market, the production of consumer goods is restricted, and great hardship is the consequence.

Technological progress frequently results in more unemployment rather than an easing of the burden of work for all. The profit motive, in conjunction with competition among capitalists, is responsible for an instability in the accumulation and utilization of capital [money, machines] *which leads to an increasingly severe depression. Unlimited competition leads to a huge waste of labor, and to the crippling of the social consciousness of individuals."*

—Albert Einstein

CHAPTER 9
The Resource-Management Database

The resource-management database (RMD) divides, subdivides, and categorizes each vocation as finely as possible into specific knowledge skill sets. Engineering is an example of a knowledge skill set that has subdivisions: civil, mechanical, chemical, and so on. Each engineering division can be further subdivided and categorized at the sub-subdivision levels.

Our personal records within the RMD can be updated to reflect such items as present field of study, or present area of employment. Additionally, our expected graduation dates, intended retirement dates, and other aspects of our curricula vitae can all be contained and updated in the RMD.

Therefore, the number of people working in each knowledge skill set, along with work times, salaries, and locations, can all be ascertained from the RMD. Thereby, students trying to decide their future direction can use the RMD to see what fields have too many or too few workers.

Skill sets and areas with a shortage of labor would offer higher-than-average wages. Skill sets and areas with a surplus of labor would have lower-than-average wages. The RMD can even show how many students have already registered for a particular field of study, and how this would affect the future job market and wages for each area in the future. So that an accurate picture of the employment sector can be made in advance.

Usually, when someone loses their job, they are given at least one month's notice. This information can also be entered into the RMD. On the first of each month, the RMD sends out a text message.

An example message could read:

> *"We have good news everyone. Thanks to new labor-saving and cost-reducing technologies; next month we can all work less and produce more. The RMD shows that starting next month, 2 percent of the workforce might not have employment. To avoid a 2 percent tax on your income, consider working 2 percent less time—so that we can all have a job. Don't worry, we can all work 2 percent less because the cost of living also just became 2 percent less as well."*

In a free economy production has only one cost—people time. No more extortion costs. If the same level of production requires 2 percent less labor overall, then overall everything also costs 2 percent less as well.

For the example of 2 percent unemployment, every employer would have thirty days to add 2 percent to their employment roster, in order to avoid a 2 percent tax to his or her income starting the following month. If an employer has fifty employees, then that would mean adding one more to the roster.

This tax could be called the labor-distribution tax (LDT). Money from the labor-distribution tax is transferred as a salary to those not employed and studying full-time, as explained in the previous section. On an individual level, each person would try to work 2 percent less time. Not from any legal restrictions or requirements, but only to avoid paying a 2 percent LDT starting the following month.

Managers can leave it for each employee to decide for him or herself. Whether to work a day, for which someone else would receive the payment; or, take a day off, and let someone else work the day, since others would receive the payment for it anyway.

The LDT gives everyone a clear choice. With 2 percent unemployment, workers can give 2 percent of their work time in the form of a 2 percent tax taken from their salaries; or, they can give 2 percent of their work time literally, by working 2 percent less time. But one way or the other, 2 percent unemployment will take away 2 percent of workers' work time—either as a tax— or as actual time on the job.

Most likely many workers will opt for working less time. In this way there will be a natural reduction in individual work hours as we make informed choices and try to avoid taxes. This labor-distribution system offers many social and economic benefits. We would never worry again about losing our jobs. Most importantly, it provides a way for the economy to shed unproductive and counterproductive jobs.

Examples of counterproductive jobs are telemarketers who trick elderly people into buying things they don't need and don't want. Then there's the daily mail saying we won millions of dollars, if only we send fifty dollars first.

And engineers who are tasked with making cars, phones, and lightbulbs, to last only so long before failing. Engineered obsolescence is common in manufacturing. And then there are drug traffickers, scams, theft, and all manner of criminal endeavors.

These are examples of unproductive labor. There are many unproductive and counterproductive jobs in our economy! Unproductive jobs do not generate wealth, and counterproductive jobs destroy wealth.

We can either let others in to work along with us, so that we can work less and earn more; or, we force others to work against us, forcing us in turn to work more and earn less.

It's a very true saying that "many hands make light work."

While there will always be those who try to get something for nothing, most people prefer to be gainfully employed in a productive job. With this labor-distribution system, productive people can let go of those unproductive and sometimes even criminal jobs, and know for sure that productive jobs, and productive people, will find a match. Given the proper training and a fair chance, many criminals might even find mainstream jobs more attractive.

Some analysts suggest that some people are mentally or emotionally challenged, or otherwise handicapped, and are unable to work in a productive job. Some say welfare or criminal jobs are all they can do.

There is a lesson that speaks to this issue. It is

something I heard directly from the very famous and great author Doctor Deepak Chopra MD. It is the story of a boy who grew up in an abusive home environment. As a result, by the age of nine this boy had developed acute schizophrenia and needed to be institutionalized.

Jump ahead five years and a new doctor arrives at this institute. For some inexplicable reason this doctor feels a connection with the boy. By this point, the boy had lost his ability to speak and have control over his bodily functions. He was lost forever.

Nevertheless, the doctor was compelled to seek legal guardianship of the boy. He took the boy out of the institute and gave him a home and a caring family. Within just a few weeks from arriving at his new home, the boy was able to speak simple words.

That same boy went on to become a medical doctor and now lives in a million-dollar home with his wife and 3 children. This story tells the whole story about life, love, and the healing power of acceptance. Doctor Chopra mentions this story in one of his earlier books.

The moral of the story: often people just need a fighting chance. Most people want to live up to their own and others expectations, but sometimes life's obstacles can be too much for us and we succumb to them.

We may not be able to give all of the down trodden in life, the love and wisdom of a very great man and that of his family, but we can give the next best thing. We can give everyone a good education and a productive job. Given that, many people can heal themselves just fine. Provided the environment is not so "dog eat dog" competitive.

Competition can be good fun, when it's about who

gets the corner office or a trophy on their mantel. But when it's about who gets to have a job, a home, and a family, then the competition has become too serious to call it just— "a little friendly competition".

Then we have to expect things like ISIS and random shootings to take expression in the world. A world largely without heart or reason for far too many.

I am reminded of the story of the Lupoe family during the 2008 financial crisis. The mother and father of this family both worked as nurses at the same hospital. The Lupoe family was buried alive under a mountain of debt. They were one of the millions that had fallen prey to the low interest teaser scams that were so common back then.

They tried to deal with their debt problems by falsifying their income statements with child care services (to get less expensive child care). When their employer found out about this, they terminated them both—literally!

A few months later this family was about to lose their home. Something they had worked very hard over most of their lives to build up. Faced with the reality that he, his wife, and his five children (all under the age of eight—with two sets of twins) would soon be living on the street, and with no hope in sight; he killed his wife, his five children, and then himself.

Others less forgiving might have thought to visit a few Wall Street bankers first. If only to remind the living to think things through a little more carefully—before destroying other people's lives.

While this was happening, executives at Goldman Sacks and other banks across the United States were giving themselves huge multi-million dollar Christmas bonuses.

I remember a news article explaining that all the bank bonuses that Christmas was more than enough to cover the *workout* cost for all the homes in foreclosure across the U.S.

The *workout cost* is the amount of money a mortgagor has fallen behind in his mortgage payments. You would think that the bankers would have felt a little responsible for causing millions of families to lose everything they had worked for over most of their lives.

Perhaps bankers could have settled for their multi-million dollar salaries, and forgo millions more in bonuses; so that millions of families could have kept their homes that Christmas (and many more Christmases). This would have also had the side benefit of stopping a financial (and humanitarian) catastrophe from engulfing the world.

Keep in mind that the government (via the Fed) was able to come up with $5 trillion dollars of new government money (QE), plus $700 billion dollars of tax payers' money—in order to save the bankers from themselves.

All those trillions could have been saved, if only a tiny fraction of that money had been used to pay the workout cost instead. And then the whole world could have been saved from the bankers, and not just a few bankers.

Additionally, mortgages could have been restructured, by returning them to their low interest teaser rates. Considering that governments (via their central banks) can give bankers negative interest rates, and trillions of new government QE money, then governments can do and give anything they want to—but only for a few bankers it would seem.

Why are bankers responsible for the financial crisis of 2008?

There is a very long list of reasons why, but I will only mention a few here. Bankers have a fiduciary responsibility to check the soundness of loans before making them. Because they are not lending out their own money. They are lending out our money on deposit, and our money made new by our government.

Bankers were not only making loans to people that could not possibly afford them, but also making predatory loans. Loans with low interest teaser rates upfront, and the real rates soon to come seldom talked about, or talked around as manageable through refinancing. This was not only misleading, but in some cases, outright fraud.

After a few years of the low teaser rates, then the real high rates kicked in for the next twenty-five years.

And then there were ninja mortgages—no income and no job. Everyone needs to see the biopic "The Big Short". Truly is a must see for everyone and also very entertaining! That is unless, you are among of the millions of families that lost your homes—then this movie may only make you angry!

Rest in peace little Lupoe family. As we speak, tens of millions of families all over the world are trapped in their own personal hells; with no way out, and little hope fading fast. Not unlike the way Lupoe family suffered at the end. And if it happened to the Lupoe family—then it could happen to many more of us.

A mayor of California said, *"A man who recently lost his job allowed the despair to put him over the edge. Unfortunately, this has been an all-too-common story in the last few months. But that does not, and should not, lead people to resort to desperate measures.*

A man killed his ex-wife, her parents and friends at a Christmas party in West Covina last month after losing his job. In October, a 45-year-old father of three shot and killed his wife and children in their Porter Ranch home after describing financial stress in a suicide note."

The mayor urged residents experiencing financial stress to talk to friends and neighbors and seek counseling. While the mayor was saying these words, six-hundred-thousand Americans were losing their jobs every month. *"Hotlines and an open heart",* will not give families back their homes or their jobs.

One total moron and a Fox news contributor, commented that the Lupoe family's suicide note[13] sounded *"rambling and crazy".* When you are about to end the life of everyone you hold dear, followed by ending your own life. I expect you will not be firing on all eight cylinders. Please try to imagine the emotional toll, anguish, and torment that he, and they, must have been going through at that moment. I am only astonished that he was able to write anything at all.

Only Michelle Mockin would be so stupid as to ridicule the prose of a suicide note left by an entire family. It was just that kind of heartless callus that got the Lupoe family murdered. And who knows how many more murdered? Not to mention millions more homeless.

Unproductive Jobs

In London Ontario, November 2008, the police were called in and a man was charged for feeding the squirrels in a city park. Apparently, the architects of this bylaw were concerned that some squirrels may have nut allergies.

Picture a very large room filled with administrators. They are sitting around an enormous conference table. Everyone is looking around at each other in silence and wondering what to do.

Someone jumps up excited. The person says, *"I've got it. We can make a new law that stops people from feeding the squirrels!"*

Another person chimes in and says, *"That's brilliant. It sidesteps the save-the-whale people completely. We'll still need some spin on this; we can say that it's for the squirrels' protection.*

Just think of all the focus groups, the studies, environmental-impact assessments, regulatory and legislative oversight—we have a lot of work to do."

And if the above scenario seems far-fetched, then consider the next section.

How a Problem Is Perpetuated

The federal and provincial governments of Canada were developing a device to monitor a nuclear reactor. The device was to carry cameras, probes, and other tools through very long sections of pipe, around elbows, and through weld penetrations.

In some of Canada's early nuclear reactors, standard metal U-bolts were used to brace metal pipes. There was a concern that hydrostatic shaking of the pipes would cause fretting against the U-bolts, which could result in a leak, or leaks, deep inside the reactor vault, or the Calandria as it is called in Canada.

A student was brought to the reactor for his first day of orientation. The director of the facility proudly displayed the results of two years of research and development efforts. He called it the Robot Worm. It consisted of three balloons connected in a line by hoses, valves, and gaskets. Under microprocessor control, the balloons inflated and deflated rhythmically to move like a worm through pipes.

The director mentioned that the Robot Worm was still not able to support a payload. In other words, the balloons could move through the pipes, but they could not carry the cameras and other tools needed for the monitoring and repair.

Upon hearing this, the student interrupted his orientation to suggest an alternative: a single balloon with an air hose attached. The air hose served to inflate and deflate the balloon, while also pulling a payload behind it.

The student further described a mechanism by which the balloon could be inflated inside the pipe to create a partial seal. Air was then pumped into the pipe to move the balloon like a piston in a cylinder (the pipe representing the cylinder). In addition, the balloon could expand, contract, and change shape as necessary to negotiate the elbows and weld penetrations.

The student called his idea a Balloon Piston. Upon hearing the student's idea, the director closed his office door for privacy. He asked the student to make a Balloon Piston for testing. That weekend, the student was sent to Toronto to test the device in a life-sized mock-up.

The Balloon Piston met and exceeded all design

requirements, but it was never used. Nor was it ever mentioned again—by the director's orders. Instead, it sat in a box in the director's office and the student spent the next four months of his first-year co-op engineering work term assisting in the development of the Robot Worm.

Why was the Balloon Piston put away? As the director explained, "We'll be riding the money train for years on this one." However, he kept the functional Balloon Piston on hand in the unlikely event that "we ever get a call that there is a leak."

Money for research is granted only for as long as the problem is not solved. This may partly explain why we still have so many problems. Two years had already been spent developing the Robot Worm. Three years later, the Robot Worm was still in development, and it still could not support a payload.

The labor-distribution system presented here, offers a way for everyone to voluntarily stop their unproductive and counterproductive jobs, and instead help with making homes, cars, and all the other things we really want and need. We would all work less from the added human resources, and yet earn more because, per person, more would be produced from the added workers making useful things.

Furthermore, as time goes on, robots will do even more for us. A system is needed that will allow the labor market to adapt dynamically to changing labor conditions and demands, while also ensuring that we all have the best possible training and good productive jobs.

CONCLUSION

We have reason to be hopeful. Although past civilizations carried on as they did for thousands of years, during the past few hundred years, a few good ideas have been tested and found to be true.

It is up to us now to move forward. We can allow the present system to continue, or we can make specific changes that will guide society in a new direction, and ensure an even brighter future for ourselves, our children, their children, and generations to come.

Postscript

We've all come thousands of years and millions of miles together. We are almost there. After just three more steps we are home free.

Step 1: Read this book.
Step 2: Get two friends to read this book in a one-month span.
Step 3: Help each other to understand and wait a short time.

This creates a geometric progression: one, three, six, twelve, twenty-four, forty-eight, and so on. Once enough people have read this book, more information can come to light.

Everyone is always telling me that the world cannot be changed, but the funny thing is that's all I ever see the world do is change. Change is the only constant. If the world is going to change regardless of what we do, then why not try to bring change for the better?

Should we resign ourselves to be worse? Can we leave this world a better place? For better or worse, only you can answer this question!

"Money is the most important subject intellectual persons can investigate and reflect upon. It is so important that our present civilization may collapse unless it is widely understood and its defects remedied very soon."

—Robert H. Hemphill, circa 1939, Federal Reserve Bank of Atlanta

*"There were some who saw it coming [the 2008 financial crisis]. While the whole word was having a big old party. A few outsiders and weirdos saw what no one else could. These outsiders saw the giant lie at the heart of the economy, and they saw it by doing something that the rest of the suckers never thought to do—**they looked**."*

—Opening scene of the Biopic *The Big Short*

"He only has the right to criticize who has the heart to help."

—Abraham Lincoln

"A theft of greater magnitude and still more ruinous, is the making of paper money; it is greater because in this money there is absolutely no real value; it is more ruinous because by its gradual depreciation during the time of its existence, it produces the effect which would be proration of the coins. All those iniquities are founded on the false idea the money is but a sign."

—Count Destutt de Tracy, 1754-1836

ADDENDUM A

Our Banking System in More Detail

A New Beginning

To explain our banking system in greater detail, we go to the island nation of Grenada. Grenada has finished a national referendum and has decided to start over new. The government of Grenada has just issued a new currency, where everyone is given ten thousand new Grenada dollars.

Note: for the purpose of this discussion, Grenada currency is also named dollars and uses the dollar sign ($).

At the start, there is only one bank; it is aptly named the First Bank. Later we will generalize this discussion to include many banks. All Grenadians deposit their new cash in the First Bank.

Grenada has a population of exactly one hundred thousand, and everyone is over the age of sixteen and has a bank account. This gives the First Bank exactly $1 billion of new first-tier money to work with.

First-tier money is made by the government, usually

through a central bank. The $1 billion of new first-tier money is a liability to the First Bank, because it represents money potentially owed to depositors, if depositors opt to withdraw their money on deposit.

However, the $1 billion on deposit is also an asset to the First Bank, because the bank can use this money to buy more assets. Banking laws require banks to balance assets to equal liabilities (deposits). Therefore, a bank can always sell its assets in order to return all deposits to all depositors.

The First Bank has total liabilities of $1 billion: $1 billion of first-tier money on deposit from one hundred thousand depositors.

The First Bank also has total assets of $1 billion: $1 billion of first-tier money on deposit from one hundred thousand depositors.

The First Bank's assets equal its liabilities, as required by banking laws.

Someone on Granada wants to buy a home. However, the home costs $500,000, but everyone has only $10,000 to his or her name. However, the First Bank has $1 billion at its disposal.

This is the value and service that banks provide to society. Banks allow people and businesses to buy things that otherwise would not be possible for us to have, and pay for them later over an extended period of time.

The bank can easily lend out $500,000 from its stash of $1 billion. This loan is facilitated as an asset purchase by the First Bank. The bank is buying something of value from the would be home buyer. The bank is buying a signed contract. A type of bond that has lots of little payments along the way—rather than one big payment at the end—called a mortgage.

The home buyer is agreeing to let the home be used as collateral against the loan. The mortgage is an asset that can later be sold by the bank if it chooses. The monthly mortgage payments go to the owner of the mortgage. If a home buyer defaults on his mortgage, then the home also goes to the owner of the mortgage. A mortgage is an asset sold by the home buyer to the bank in exchange for $500,000.

The home buyer uses this $500,000 gained from the sale of the mortgage (to the bank) to buy a home. The home seller deposits this $500,000 into the bank for safekeeping. The bank gets the mortgage, the home buyer gets the home, and the home seller gets the $500,000.

Note that the amount of money in the bank has not changed from this home purchase because the $500,000 never left the bank. Because the money cannot leave the bank. Because there is only the one bank.

The bank still has $1 billion in its vault. Until the government creates more first-tier money, the $1 billion in the First Bank is an immutable constant. However, total deposits have now increased by $500,000 to $1 billion plus $500,000 on deposit.

The First Bank's total liabilities (deposits) now equal $1 billion $500,000: $1 billion of first-tier money on deposit from one hundred thousand depositors, and now also $500,000 on deposit from one home seller.

The First Bank's total assets now also equal $1 billion $500,000: $1 billion of first-tier money on deposit from one hundred thousand depositors, and now also a $500,000 mortgage bond.

The First Bank's assets equal its liabilities, as required by banking laws.

Note that there is now $500,000 dollars more on deposit than what the bank has in its vault to cover it (deposits). However, now the bank also has a mortgage (bond) worth $500,000 that it can sell so as to redeem all deposits to all depositors (if need be).

When the First Bank purchased a bond-asset for $500,000, this also had the effect of creating $500.000 of new second-tier money. Second-tier money is the money that banks create as a by-product of purchasing assets with first-tier money. At this point the First Bank has $1 billion of first-tier money on deposit, and $500,000 of second-tier money on deposit. For total deposits of $1 billion $500,000.

The terms *first-tier* and *second-tier* money are not in standard use, they are used by some educators to explain our banking and monetary system—as we do now.

Another person sells a mortgage to the bank for $500,000. The seller of the mortgage, who is also the buyer of the home, uses this $500,000 to buy a home. The seller of the home deposits this $500,000 into the bank for safekeeping.

Now the bank has total deposits of $1 billion plus $1 million, but still only $1 billion in its vault. The government has yet to make more new money. At this point the bank has $1 billion of first-tier money on deposit, and $1 million of second-tier money on deposit. For total deposits of $1 billion plus $1 million.

In purchasing another $500,000 mortgage asset, the First Bank also created another $500,000 of second-tier money. The new (bank-made) second-tier money goes to the seller of the asset—in this case, the would be home buyer.

The home buyer uses this $500,000 to buy a home. The home seller deposits this $500,000 into the bank for safekeeping. So no money leaves the bank, because there is still only the one bank. Later we will generalize this discussion to include many banks, but for now we continue with only the one bank. Until the government makes more new money, first-tier money levels can only remain constant at $1 billion.

The First Bank's constant inexhaustible reservoir of $1 billion of first-tier money can be reused again and again like this to buy more assets. Until, the bank has total bond-assets of $19 billion—and therefore also $19 billion of new bank made deposits—from the sale of thirty-eight thousand homes, at an average cost of $500,000 per home.

The *fractional reserve* banking system then rests further asset purchases. Only a small fraction (5 percent, or $1 billion in this case) of total deposits ($20 billion in this case) is held on reserve to fulfill potential withdrawals.

However, should more withdraws be necessary, the bank also has $19 billion of mortgage assets that it can sell, so as to redeem all deposits to all depositors if need be.

Note that the First Bank started with only $1 billion, and turned it into $20 billion, by purchasing $19 billion of mortgage assets. And in so doing, the bank also created $19 billion of new deposits—from the sale of thirty-eight thousand homes, at an average cost of $500,000 per home.

Now the First Bank has $1 billion of first-tier money

on deposit, and $19 billion of second-tier money on deposit; for total deposits of $20 billion.

This is called the *money multiplier effect* of the *fractional reserve* system. If banking rules instead required a 10 percent *reserve requirement*, then this would facilitate only a ten-times (10X) *money multiplier effect*. A 3 percent *reserve requirement* would allow for a thirty-three-times (33X) *money multiplier effect* and so on.

Note that if everyone attempts to takeout all their money from the First Bank, then only the first 5 percent to reach the bank can take all their money out, and the rest would get nothing. This is called a *bank run*. Alternatively, everyone can get back 5 percent of what they have on deposit.

Even if all assets are sold, in an attempt to return all despots to all depositors, still only 5 percent of all deposits can be recovered. This is because there is still only $1 billion in existence (on Granada), and still only the First Bank that thinks it has $20 billion in deposits. In a way, second-tier money does not really exist, except in bankers' imaginations and wishful thinking.

Therefore, the *fractional reserve* banking system represents a kind of Ponzi scheme. It is criminal, but somehow made legal by our politicians. It's criminal also because it allows bankers to make new second-tier money for themselves as they purchase assets. If we make new money for ourselves as we buy stuff, then it's called counterfeiting—and we go to prison fast.

The First Bank having reached a 5 percent *reserve requirement*, requires more first-tier money before it can make further asset purchases. So the First Bank borrows more first-tier money from the central bank.

Only the central bank can make more first-tier money. And only banks can borrow new first-tier money from the central bank. Note that new first-tier money is created by our government, and therefore really belongs to our government. And through our government, it really belongs to all of us.

With this additional $1 billion of new first-tier money, the bank is able to purchase an additional $19 billion of new assets, while also remaining compliant to a 5 percent *reserve requirement.*

Next the First Bank purchases $1 billion of ABC Inc. (5 percent of ABC). With this new asset purchase, no money leaves the First Bank, because there are no other banks for the money to exit to—yet.

The bank still has $2 billion of first-tier money in its vault. Recall that just prior to the latest asset purchase, the bank added $1 billion of new first-tier money to its reserves by borrowing $1 billion from the central bank.

The assets purchased belong to the bank, and not to the depositors or the government who supplied the money to make asset purchases possible. Hence, depositors and our government (we) take most of the risk, while banks take most of the reward.

The First Bank now owns $1 billion of ABC Inc. (an asset to the bank), and ABC now has $1 billion on deposit in the First Bank (an asset to ABC, but a liability to the bank).

The First Bank's total liabilities now equal $22 billion: $1 billion of first-tier money on deposit from one hundred thousand depositors, $1 billion of first-tier money on loan from the central bank, $19 billon on deposit from thirty-eight thousand home sellers, and now also $1 billion on deposit in the account of ABC, from the sale of 5 percent of ABC to the First Bank.

The First Bank's total assets now also equal $22 billion: $1 billion of first-tier money from one hundred thousand depositors, $1 billion of first-tier money from the central bank, $19 billion of mortgage-bonds, and $1 billion of ABC stock.

The First Bank's assets equal its liabilities, as required.

When the First Bank purchased $1 billion of ABC stock, it created an additional $1 billion of new second-tier money on deposit in the account of ABC at the First Bank. Second-tier money is created by banks as they buy assets with first-tier money.

The new (bank-made) second-tier money goes to the seller of the assets, and the assets purchased go to the bank. Initially, the assets purchased have the same dollar value as the second-tier money that was created to buy them (the assets), but over time, the money loses its value because of inflation. In contrast, the companies and other assets purchased with (bank-made) second-tier money appreciate in value over time.

Some stocks have dividend payments, and all stocks have retained earnings. Therefore, it is far more valuable to get the assets purchased with new (bank-made) second-tier money, than it is to get the new money that did the purchasing. Besides, the assets can always be converted to money at any time by simply selling them.

The First Bank dips again into its inexhaustible well of first-tier money to buy another billion-dollars of ABC stock. This adds another $1 billion to ABC's deposit account at the First Bank. ABC Inc. now has $2 billion on deposit at the First Bank.

The First Bank's total liabilities now equal $23 billion: $1 billion of first-tier money on deposit from one hundred thousand depositors, $1 billion of first-tier money on loan from the central bank, $19 billion on deposit from thirty-eight thousand home sellers, and $2 billion on deposit in the account of ABC (from ABC having sold $2 billion of ownership to the First Bank).

The First Bank's total assets now also equal $23 billion: $1 billion of first-tier money from one hundred thousand depositors, 1 billion of first-tier money from the central bank, $19 billion in mortgage-bonds, and $2 billion of ABC stock.

The First Bank's assets equal its liabilities, as required.

The First Bank can continue to purchase more assets like this until it owns $19 billion of ABC Inc. The First Bank is then *fully leveraged* once again. This keeps 5 percent (or $2 billion in this case) of total deposits ($40 billion in this case) "on reserve" with first-tier money. Once again, the First Bank rests further assets purchases until it has more first-tier money to work with.

Asset Appreciation

Suppose after five years, the ABC asset owned by the First Bank is worth $39 billion (up from $19 billion initially). The ABC asset has roughly doubled in value over five years. However, the purchase price or the amount that was deposited into ABC's account at the time of purchase can only remain constant at $19 billion.

Banking laws only require banks to balance their assets to equal their liabilities (deposits). However, now the value of the First Bank's assets exceeds the value of its liabilities by $20 billion. Therefore, the owners of the First Bank can transfer ownership of $20 billion of assets away from their bank and over to themselves.

The owners of the First Bank can then keep or sell these assets and pocket $20 billion. This is over and above what bankers profit from interest charges and dividend payments. To put this into perspective, Apple Inc. went from being a $100 million company in 1980, to a $700 billion company in 2015.

Microsoft, General Electric, and thousands of other companies have all seen similar asset appreciations. This gives a little glimpse as to why many company assets are often held by private banks—to keep this extreme level of profiteering hidden.

As assets appreciate above their initial sale price, bankers tend to sell their assets to hardworking people like you and me. Bankers often to sell at *point of profit* when indicated. Companies tend to follow a known life cycle that is carefully studied.

However, the one asset class that bankers tend to hold on to is oil and other natural resource-based companies, but this could change as oil loses its dominance, and as developing nations near their destinations and slow down.

Second Bank and More

Now we introduce a second bank into the discussion, aptly named the Second Bank. The question is, what will happen to first-tier money levels at each bank now that we have two banks in the system?

For the banking system to continue to work as before, we need to show that first-tier money levels will remain constant at each bank. Just as first-tier money levels remained constant when we had only the First Bank. We need to show that each bank will have its own inexhaustible well of first-tier money to draw upon for making asset purchases.

For the sake of having easy numbers to work with, we change the population of Grenada from one hundred thousand to three hundred thousand. Further, we suppose that the First Bank has two hundred thousand depositors, and the Second Bank has the other one hundred thousand depositors. Take note of the two-to-one ratio of customers at the First Bank, to customers at the Second Bank.

Someone in Grenada is selling his car. Suppose he gets an average of three calls a day from potential buyers. Of the three callers, chances are that two will be with the First Bank, and one with the Second Bank. The following day all three callers might be with one bank or the other.

However, as the days add up, it should tend to average out to two potential buyers from the First Bank, and one from the Second Bank. Simply because there are twice as many people with the First Bank as the Second Bank. It is twice as likely that the buyer will end up being with the First Bank.

Now envision thousands of sellers and buyers, and thousands of cars. And it's not just cars—but all the things we buy and sell every day. And it's not just one day, but forever. So as the numbers get larger, and the time interval grows to eternity, the law of large numbers, averages, and probabilities take hold.

The First Bank has twice as many buyers as the Second Bank. Money leaves the buyer's bank to flow into the seller's bank. With the First Bank having twice as many buyers, money will be flowing out from the First Bank, twice as fast as it flows out from the Second Bank.

At this rate, soon the First Bank will be emptied of all its money, and the Second Bank will have all the money. Where else can the money go—if there are only these two banks? We only need to consider the other side of the equation to resolve this conundrum.

For every buyer, there must also be a seller. Just as the First Bank has twice as many buyers, so it also has twice as many sellers. With selling money leaves the buyers bank to go into the sellers bank. With the First Bank having twice as many sellers, money will be flowing into the First Bank twice as fast as it flows into the Second Bank.

Hence, money is flowing into the First Bank twice as fast, but it is also flowing out twice as fast. Therefore, inflow equals outflow. When inflow equals outflow, money levels can only remain constant at each bank. Additionally, the sum total of all first-tier money for both banks combined can only remain constant—just as it did in the one-bank scenario.

In other words, there are mathematical forces in play that tend to keep first-tier money levels constant at each bank, just as it remained constant in the one-bank scenario. As a result, each bank has its own inexhaustible source of first-tier money to draw upon for making asset purchases. This does not take into account special circumstances—such as *bank runs*.

Minor fluctuations of a bank's first-tier money levels can occur over time. And if an imbalance persists, then a bank simply offers promotions, such as better lending or saving rates to bring more customers, and their money—back into their bank. However, time, probability, and statistics, do most of the heavy lifting in this balancing act.

As each bank purchases assets, it does not deplete or reduce each bank's first-tier money reserves. Rather, first-tier money levels tend to remain constant over time, while assets and deposits accumulate with each new asset purchase.

The preceding analysis readily lends itself to many banks. What is true for two banks, is also true for three banks—by *inspection*. And what is true for two and three banks, must also hold true for four banks and so on—by *induction*.

There is perhaps another reason why the *money multiplier effect* (and its harmful results) have been so overlooked by so many. It may be related to how the *fractional reserve* banking system is introduced in schools and universities. The standard example used by many educators goes something like the following.

Someone deposits $1,000 dollars into a bank. Of this $1,000, the bank keeps $50 dollars on reserve, and loans out the other $950 dollars. This is where most educators tend to stop with this example. It is only meant to explain (by example) that 5% of deposits are held on reserve to fulfill potential withdraws. It is not intended to explain the deeper nuances of the *fractional reserve* banking system.

This example can be misleading. It can give the idea that with $1,000 dollars (borrowed or deposited), a bank buys only $950 dollars of assets. But note, if there is only one bank, then the $950 dollars never even leaves the bank. The bank still has the $1,000 on reserve, and not only $50 as this example would suggest.

This constant reserve dynamic also happens for two banks, and likewise for three banks as explained previously. And if this constant reserve dynamic is preserved for two and three banks, then it must also hold true for four banks and so on—by *induction*.

If banks purchase only $950 dollars of assets, for every $1,000 deposited or borrowed, then there would be no *money multiplier effect*. However, it is commonly understood and accepted that banks do multiply the money supply 20 to 30 times, depending on the reserve requirement. And this is called the *money multiplier effect* of the *fractional reserve system*.

However, even if it was the case (which it is not) that for every $1,000 dollars (deposited or borrowed), a bank buys only $950 dollars of assets. Take note that the $1,000 dollars is either from our money on deposit, or from our money borrowed from our central bank.

Whether the $1,000 comes from our deposits, or from our central bank, it is still all our money buying assets for banks. Laws of business and commerce would dictate that the people supplying the money and also taking the risk—should likewise receive the reward, and not only a few financiers using other people's money to buy assets.

And let's not forget, there is still the issue of banks having first access to IPO companies as they are sold. And exclusive access to new government money as it is made by our central bank with QE and overnight lending.

So whichever viewpoint you side with on this technical issue, it does not alter the overall premise or validity of this book.

For those sceptics out there who need to see proof of the money multiplier effect in action, a classical simulation is provided with note 14 in the notes section at the back of this book.

We now have enough background knowledge to talk about what happened in 2008.

The Financial Crisis of 2008

Leading up to the crash of 2008, a substantial portion of banks' assets relating to mortgages—and later to equities in general—lost their value. This changed the value of total assets owned by banks.

As a group, banks' liabilities then exceeded the value of their assets by many trillions of dollars. Considering that the equity market in the United States went from a value of $25 trillion down to only $13 trillion—obviously, it was going to take many trillions of dollars to fix this mess.

This condition triggers banking regulations and protocols that would have shut offending banks down, and started an asset-liquidation process so as to return all deposits to all depositors—or as much as possible to as many as possible.

The real problem was that bankers did not want to put money back into their banks. The same money that bank owners took out from their banks as assets went up in value over their initial sale prices.

When assets go up in value 20 percent a year, bank

owners can move 20 percent a year away from their banks, and over to their own personal bank accounts. When asset values went down in value for a change, the bank owners did not want to put any of that money back into their banks. Instead, bankers forced us to foot the bill with a bailout.

The first thing the United States and European governments did to deal with the financial crisis, was change the "market-to-market" accounting rules. Banks were no longer required by law to use the current market value of assets when doing their books. Instead, bankers were allowed to use the same prices they had paid for their assets at the time of purchase; or, the current market value, whichever was greater.

With the stroke of a pen, total assets at all banks suddenly balanced up to equal total deposits. Of course, it was only true on paper. That measure bought some time and stopped the closing and liquidation of many of the biggest banks, perhaps even all banks when collateral damage is considered.

However, if bankers had done this accounting trick on their own, without first getting the nod-wink from government, then bankers would have gone to jail for banking fraud. This is also known as cooking the books.

This stopgap measure was only a cheat and a fraud, and did nothing to fix the underlying imbalance of assets to liabilities. Therefore, many governments also came up with their own version of TARP (Troubled Asset Relief Program).

For the United States this meant $700 billion-dollars of taxpayers' money was used to buy up bad assets from banks.

However, $700 billion was a drop in the proverbial ocean. Many trillions would be needed to recapitalize all banks, and rebalance assets to equal liabilities (deposits). But where could they find people with trillions of dollars, who were also stupid enough to buy assets priced way above market value?

That's when and where we came in. Through our government (our central bank), we purchased those troubled assets from banks by the trillions. They called it *quantitative easing* (QE) and held press conferences to tell everyone all about it. They acted like it was a good thing.

New money created by our central bank is a public asset that belongs to all of us. Politicians could have used the same TARP and Fed QE money to insist on more bank ownership. The government could have even insisted on total ownership of many of the biggest banks, and majority ownership on what was left. Otherwise, all banks would have died a painful death.

That was our big chance to restore balance in the economy and create a proper legal framework for our financial system. That is how our banking system should have been structured right from the start—before governments started creating new money through central banks. For more on this, read addendum C: *A New Financial Model.*

Any private investor (such as Warren Buffett) would have invested his money only in exchange for bank equity (ownership) and would have steered clear of buying toxic assets from banks, especially if those assets were priced well above their fair market value.

If central banks had paid fair market value for troubled assets, it would have done nothing to rebalance banks' assets to equal their liabilities, and thereby recapitalize banks. Banks could have easily sold for themselves their troubled assets on the open market at the current market value.

It would have moved bank asset ownership away from stocks and bonds to holding more of the money-asset. However, the money-asset would have the same dollar value, as the assets sold to generate the money. This would have done nothing to increase the dollar value of total assets, so as to equal total liabilities (deposits).

Banks needed to sell their bad assets at prices well above their true market value to rebalance assets to equal liabilities, but where could they find buyers that stupid or generous? Not one person in Congress would have done that with his or her own money, but they did it with ours.

The Fed rejects the notion that with QE money it was buying assets off banks, and at prices above fair market value. The Fed insists that it was buying assets from the *secondary market* (a.k.a. the *open* or *public* market), and not directly from banks, as is usually the way among banks.

First of all, banks can sell their assets on the *open* market, just as easily as the Fed can buy those same assets on the same *secondary market*. Just because the Fed and banks are both buying and selling their assets on the same venue, does not stop or preclude the Fed from buying assets from banks.

If banks buy and sell their bad assets back and forth to each other a few times—at prices well above their true market values— then after that, I suppose the Fed can say with a straight face that it was paying recent market-selling prices and not more. Tricky Fed.

We always have to be careful when dealing with people because every now and then they can fool you. As Honest Abe once said, "You can fool all the people some of the time, and some of the people all the time, but you cannot fool all the people all the time."

However, even if the Fed was not buying assets directly from banks—and perhaps even at the current market value—but just by the Fed and other central banks, exerting the full force of their buying power on the market, this cannot help but elevate asset values. That sustained buying pressure on the market (from QE over five years) has returned asset values to what they were before the crash of 2008.

If the central bank pays $2 billion, for an asset worth only $1 billion, then the central bank is in effect giving away $1 billion. This is charity by the billions for billionaires.

Martin Luther King said, "This is a country (the United States) that has welfare for the rich and rugged individualism for the poor." And the man knew what he was talking about. But even MLK missed the fact that it's not only the United States, every nation has welfare for the rich.

All nations have central banks, and all nations have modeled their banking systems after the European archetype. Central banks started showing up in Europe roughly three hundred years ago; shortly after the rotary printing press arrived. The royal families of Europe quickly realized that the easiest way to make money was to literally make it. They sort of became the first central bankers.

As democracies replaced monarchies, central banks began to lend their newly created money to banks, that in turn, loaned this new money to us, twenty times over by buying assets. This most likely all got decided in the same way it was decided to give tobacco companies billion-dollar subsidies. Lobbyists bought and bribed politicians to make it that way.

Bankers and Their Debts Never to Be Repaid

Throughout this addendum, I emphasized how second-tier money created by banks buying assets, was money potentially owed by all bankers to all depositors. However, second-tier money is a perpetual debt that bankers never have to repay—and never can repay.

You might think that by simply removing all your money from the bank, that this will clear the debt owed to you by your bank. And you would be correct. You would have done precisely that—but only until you deposit your money again.

All money, once created by banks buying assets, only moves from account to account, but is always someone's deposit in the end. Bank-made second-tier money becomes a perpetual debt, owed by all bankers to all depositors, but it's a debt that bankers never have to repay, and never can repay, because all money exists as deposits within banks.

Therefore, the assets purchased by (bank-made) second-tier money becomes more like a gift or charity to bankers. This is ironic when you consider that bankers have zero tolerance for us when we don't pay back our debts to them.

If by some miracle, somehow everyone was able to takeout all their money from every bank, and keep it all out, then every bank would be forced to sell off all their companies and bonds to repay all deposits to all depositors. Only then would bankers repay all their debts to depositors.

However, it is not possible in theory or practice, for everyone to remove all their money from banks. Just as it's also not possible for all banks to sell all their assets.

This is because there is twenty times as much second-tier money, as there is first-tier money. And second-tier money can only exist within banks as deposits. Only first-tier money can exist outside of banks.

At any given time, only 5 percent of second-tier money can exist outside of banks as first-tier money. As a group, the most we can ever hope to takeout from banks is 5 percent of what we have on deposit.

Alternatively, the first 5 percent to reach their banks can take all their money out, but then the rest would get nothing. Similarly, this 5 percent ratio also applies to banks.

As a group, banks can only sell 5 percent of their assets—and then no more can be sold. Likewise, only the first 5 percent (of banks) can sell all their assets, but then the rest would get nothing. In that sense, our banking system is the ultimate global Ponzi scheme and should get the slammer.

This 5 percent ratio stems from the 5 percent *reserve requirement*. That gives rise to the twenty-times *money multiplier effect*. If the *reserve requirement* was 10 percent, it would mean a ten-times (10X) *money multiplier effect*. And all the percentages in the previous few paragraphs would change from 5 percent to 10 percent.

Some analysts suggest that first-tier money exists solely as cash or coins. However, first-tier money only means money made by our government through our central bank. And second-tier money is made by banks as they buy assets with first-tier money. All cash and coins are first-tier money, but not all first-tier money are cash and coins.

With the Grenada example, the central bank could have created one hundred thousand checking accounts, and started each account with $10,000 on deposit at the central bank. All payments can then be transacted by checks and/or debit cards. Without cash or coins, it's all first-tier money.

This is called a ledger-based monetary system and ledger-based money. It would necessitate that the central bank has accounts directly with individuals and businesses, and not only with bankers exclusively as we have now.

When the First Bank opens, everyone deposits their $10,000 in the First Bank by writing checks payable to the First Bank. Banks have three types of accounts at the central bank: debit, credit, and holding accounts.

A central bank debit account holds a bank's first-tier money reserves in ledger form. Central bank credit accounts are how overnight lending of first-tier money is implemented with banks. And this also is ledger based first-tier money.

Each of the one hundred thousand debit accounts at the central bank have now gone from $10,000 down to $0 at the central bank. But from $0 up to $10,000 at the First Bank. The central bank now owes $1 billion to the First Bank, and in turn, the First Bank now owes $10,000 to each of the one hundred thousand depositors.

What happens if we withdraw money from one bank, and put it into another bank?

Behind the scenes, this is executed by transferring the same amount of money from the sending bank's debit account at the central bank, to the receiving bank's debit account at the central bank. This is all done by changing numbers in ledgers at the central bank, and no physical money is moved.

When someone buys a home for X dollars, then X dollars moves from the buying bank's debit account at the central bank, to the selling bank's debit account at the central bank. Just by changing numbers in ledgers at the central bank, and again no physical money is moved.

First-tier money exists in two forms: as ledger based money in debit and credit accounts at the central bank, and outside of the central bank as cash and coins only.

At any given moment, the central bank knows how much first-tier money is in the banking system, and also at each bank individually. Total first-tier money is simply the sum of all debit and credit accounts at the central bank, plus all cash and coins out in the world and in banks.

Quantitative Easing

Quantitative easing is when one branch of the government prints bonds, and another branch of the government (the central bank) prints a bank draft to pay for those bonds. Suppose a billion-dollar government bond is being purchased from the government.

The central bank makes a bank draft for $1 billion and gives it to the government in payment for the bond. The central bank gets the bond and the government gets the bank draft in payment.

The government deposits the bank draft into any bank. The bank redeems the bank draft with the central bank. The central bank adds $1 billion to the bank's debit account (ledger) at the central bank. And the bank adds $1 billion to the government's debt account (ledger) at the bank. This is called quantitative easing.

This is all done by adding numbers to ledgers at the bank and at the central bank, and no new physical money is printed. It puts $1 billion of new first-tier money into the banking system. Overnight lending with the central bank also does the same thing. None of it is cash or coins; it is all new ledger-based first-tier money.

Capital Requirements

Capital requirements are a slightly different way of implementing reserve requirements. Rather than a bank keeping a supply of money reserves to fulfill possible withdrawals, an equivalent supply of "tier 1 capital" reserves act to secure deposits and fulfill withdrawals.

Tier 1 capital refers to high-quality assets that can be easily sold and converted to cash. The cash can then be used to satisfy money withdrawals as needed. Tier 1 capital is held in a special holding account at the central bank. The holding account can hold anything of value to a bank: stocks, bonds, and even gold, silver, and precious gems.

There are tax incentives and other benefits for keeping reserves in the form of tier 1 capital rather than money. Not all nations have reserve requirements, but all nations have capital requirements. This is really just another way of implementing reserve requirements.

The Basel guidelines recommend that a bank's "tier 1 capital" should always equal or exceed 5 percent of "total exposure." Total exposure equates directly with total liabilities or total assets. Some banks only need to keep 3 percent of assets on reserve; others need 7 or 8 percent. It depends on the size and type of bank, and on whether or not assets are secured or deposits insured, but 5 percent represents the average.

Not all governments adhere to the Basel guidelines. The Basel guidelines are a comprehensive set of recommendations put forward by the International Basel Committee on Banking Supervision.

As a bank's assets accumulate, the bank is required to increase owners' equity, or the value of the bank, so as to equal or exceed 5 percent of total assets, or the bank's "exposure." For example, if a bank has $20 billion of assets (and hence also deposits), then the value of the bank (owners' equity) should equal or exceed $1 billion.

If a bank needs money to support withdrawals, then some of this capital is sold to generate money and fulfill withdrawals. Usually money flows into a bank as fast as it's flowing out; so money levels tend to remain constant over time (as explained earlier in this addendum). Capital reserves are a precaution seldom used, except on occasion in the short term.

Earnings versus Interest

It's not that uncommon for IPO companies to double in value in the first five years. The bank owners can then sell half their holdings and put the proceeds into a bank to earn interest. If half the holdings are sold at twice the purchase price, this gives back to the bank the same amount of money that it created to buy those holdings. Depositing the proceeds from this sale into a bank will then earn enough interest to pay the interest fees (on bank-made money) in perpetuity.

Most IPO companies will go up five to ten-times in value over a ten to twenty-year span. After such a rise, most companies then tend to plateau, but some continue to go up. However, a company only has to double in value for banks to sell half their holdings and deposit the proceeds. The proceeds can then generate enough interest to pay the interest fees on bank-made second-tier money in perpetuity.

However, I doubt that any bank would bother with such a strategy. Most companies tend to earn much more than 1 percent per year. Saving accounts usually pay less than 1 percent. It's far more valuable for the banks and their owners to just keep their companies, and use the earnings that their companies generate to pay the interest fees on bank deposits.

Negative Interest Rates

Recently, both the European Central Bank (ECB) and the Bank of Japan (BOJ) experimented with negative interest rates. Such that banks are paid interest, rather than charged interest, on the money they borrow from the central bank.

What I want to know is—when do we get negative interest rates? When will credit card companies (via banks) pass some of these negative interest rates (and new money) on to us, and pay us to keep a balance on their cards? Imagine, getting paid 19 percent per year to keep a balance. I would put a $100,000 on one card and retire. I could do the same on a few more cards and do some traveling while I'm at it. That is the alternate reality that some private bankers live in.

Negative interest rates are just another way of recapitalizing banks; not unlike quantitative easing. It is just another way to give charity by the billions to billionaires. It is welfare for the uber-rich. Don't bankers already have enough homes, cars, yachts, and jets? We should remind ourselves, half the world is somehow living on only dollar a day.

Bank Insolvency

There is a way (in theory) for all banks to sell all their assets, but it would require that the population as a whole submit all their money to hedge funds and mutual funds for them to invest it on our behalf.

The money held by funds is kept on deposit in banks; until the funds are used to purchase assets. After the funds have used all our money to buy all assets from all banks, banks would then own all of the money-asset and no more stocks or bonds.

Although, no money leaves any banks from this— nor can it. It's only that banks would then own all of the money on deposit, rather than the former depositors. And all the funds would then own all of the stocks and bonds—on our behalf.

It is possible for banks to sell all their assets, provided banks are paid for their assets.

However, if banks are required to sell all their assets, in order to return all deposits to all depositors (and not receive all deposits as payment for assets), then only 5 percent of assets can be sold.

This gives rise to a sort of theoretical limit as to how many banks can go insolvent at one time and not bring down whole banking system. If there are one hundred banks in the local economy, and each bank is roughly the same size, then the maximum number of banks that can go insolvent at one time is 5, or 5 percent.

However, in practice, I believe this percentage to be much higher. Bank-asset liquidations can take a year or more to complete (thereby practically removing the "at one time" condition). As money is gradually returned to depositors (through asset liquidation), depositors deposit their money back into banks.

Banks can then reuse this same money once again to buy more assets from the insolvent banks. The combination of time and money returning to banks, allows the banking system to absorb a must larger percentage of insolvent banks than just the theoretical limit of 5 percent.

However, in practice, complete bank-asset liquidations rarely happen. If a bank is deemed to be insolvent, then a few scenarios can play out, but complete liquidations come last. The first choice is for an insolvent bank to be split into two banks—a good bank and a bad bank.

The good bank gets all the good assets, and the bad bank gets all the bad assets. Another bank then buys the good bank and the bad bank dies a slow death. The bad banks' bad assets are sold, and whatever proceeds can be recovered usually go to the good bank.

For the United States the Federal Deposit Insurance Corporation (FDIC) makes up any money lost in this process. Banks pay a fee to the FDIC to provide this level of protection for their banking clients.

Interested readers and policy makers may refer to the following links for further reading. The first link is "positivemoney.org," which is very accessible to the average reader. The second link "sovereignmoney.eu" is a website written by Professor Dr. Joseph Huber, former chair of economics of Martin Luther University of Germany.

http://positivemoney.org/how-money-works/how-banks-create-money/
http://www.sovereignmoney.eu/21-defining-money/
https://www.youtube.com/watch?v=cKmBYXb_9-Y
https://www.youtube.com/watch?v=CvRAqR2pAgw

"Private Capital tends to become concentrated in few hands. The result is an oligarchy of private capital. The enormous power of which cannot be effectively checked even by a democratically organized political Society.

This is true since the members of legislative bodies are selected by political parties largely financed or otherwise influenced by private capitalists who, for all practical purposes, separate the electric from the legislature.

The consequence is that the representatives of the people do not in fact sufficiently protect the interests of the underprivileged sections of the population.

Moreover, under existing conditions, private capitalists inevitably control, directly or indirectly, the main sources of information (press, radio, education).

It is thus extremely difficult and indeed in most cases quite impossible, for the individual citizen to come to objective conclusions and to make intelligent use of his political rights."

—Albert Einstein

"I sincerely believe, with you, that banking establishments are more dangerous than standing armies; and that the principle of spending money to be paid by posterity, under the name of funding, is but swindling futurity on a large scale."

—Thomas Jefferson, in a letter to John Taylor in 1816

"Poverty is not an accident. Like slavery and apartheid, it is man-made and can be removed by the actions of human beings".

—Nelson Mandela.

ADDENDUM B

Quantitative Easing

Quantitative easing (QE) is where the central bank purchases assets directly, rather than banks purchasing assets with central bank money. One asset central banks purchase is a bond. Bonds are the way governments and companies borrow money. This is called *debt financing*, as compared to *equity financing* with a stock issuance. A bond is a promise of payment of a definite amount after a certain date (the mature date).

Bonds are created by governments and companies and then sold in exchange for money. Hence, the money borrowed. This money is paid back to the buyer of the bonds when the bonds *mature* or *come due*. Matured bonds are redeemed for cash by the issuer or seller of the bond.

This is paying back the money borrowed, plus interest charges. Bonds always sell for less than what they pay out after maturity. The difference in price from buying to selling represents the interest earned on the principle.

Governments borrow money in the same way as companies. Governments issue bonds or promissory notes of payment. The government sells the bonds for money. When the bonds mature, the government needs to return this money (plus interest) to the bondholders.

Some analysts have suggested that governments could borrow money directly from the central bank, instead of borrowing from banks. This would mean central banks buying government bonds directly, or *Quantitative Easing* (QE), rather than banks buying bonds using central bank or government money.

Considering that banks get the money they need to buy bonds and other assets from the central bank in the first place, why not save a step and just borrow directly from the central bank? Interest payments would then go to the central bank and back into government coffers to reduce our taxes.

When governments borrow from banks, by way of banks buying bonds rather than the central bank, interest fees then go to the banks, and ultimately to their owners, and not into government coffers to reduce our taxes. Which is strange because the money that bought those assets for the banks came from our government.

For this reason, some people might be happy that the Fed (and not banks) purchased government bonds directly during QE. However, if later the Fed sells to banks the same assets purchased during QE, now that banks are flush full with trillions of new QE money, then it is exactly the same as if the banks had bought these assets in the first place, with our central bank money.

Governments created central banks, and then granted them the power to make new money. In some cases, unlimited new money for limitless buying power.

During the financial crisis of 2008, the central bank for the United States (the Fed) was buying assets at the rate of $85 billion per month, putting roughly a trillion new dollars a year into the banking system to effectively recapitalize all banks.

For roughly five years, the Fed purchased assets at this rate. The European Central Bank (ECB) is currently doing the same QE on roughly the same scale.

At the height of the financial crisis, the aggregate liabilities of all banks exceeded aggregate assets by many trillions of dollars. Seven hundred billion dollars of taxpayer's money was used to buy troubled assets from banks, but even that was a drop in the proverbial bucket compared to what was needed to rebalance all assets to equal all liabilities at all banks.

Keep in mind that the U.S. equity market (the stock market) had gone from a value of $25 trillion down too only $13 trillion. That is $12 trillion missing from the banking system.

So central banks stepped in to buy assets by the trillions with government money—our money. They called it *quantitative easing (QE)*.

This is welfare by the billions for billionaires. Moreover, money created by central banks is in effect money made by our government, and is therefore a public asset that belongs to our government. And that means it really belongs to all of us.

The Fed now talks about its "bloated balance sheet" and the need to reduce or sell its assets at some point in the future. The Fed already has a catchy name for it: *asset normalization*. The Fed will be selling the assets purchased with QE money—most likely to banks. Who else could afford them?

Get ready for some masterful sleight of hand and spin-doctoring in the years ahead. Whatever is done, it will not be hidden. It will be fully advertised and talked about openly as asset normalization at quarterly guidance meetings and press conferences.

Who would hide something by advertising it at press conferences? They rely on people's assumptions and lack of basic understanding of our banking system. Hopefully, this book will help clear things up.

The Fed should keep those assets from QE—not Normalize—and let the earnings that those assets garner go into government coffers to reduce our taxes. Many bank owners already have enough homes, yachts, and private jets and don't need any more.

Quantitative Easing Vs Overnight Lending

Throughout this book, I have taken the stance that banks obtain more first-tier money by way of overnight lending with the central bank. This is one of the main tools used by many nations and their central banks for putting new first-tier money into the banking system and economy.

However, quantitative easing is a more prevalent

way. When a central bank buys treasury bonds from the government, the government deposits the money acquired from this into government accounts at various banks.

Any money that comes from a central bank is new first-tier money. Once that new money is deposited into government accounts, it becomes available for banks to use and reuse twenty times over by way of purchasing assets.

From there, this new first-tier money spreads to all banks via intra-bank lending. So banks do not need to borrow new first-tier money directly from the central bank, when they can borrow it indirectly from other banks with government deposit accounts.

In time, governments spend this new first-tier money to become the paychecks and deposits of millions of government employees. Gradually, new first-tier money from QE spreads to all banks—without the need for intra-bank lending in the short-term.

From 2009 to 2014, the Fed put roughly $5 trillion new dollars of first-tier money into the banking system and economy. Essentially, giving this new money to banks to reuse twenty times over. In time, this will allow banks to purchase up to $100 trillion dollars of companies and bonds that go to the banks, and ultimately to their owners. This represents charity by the billions to billionaires that never has to be repaid.

"Whenever you find yourself on the side of the majority, it is time to pause and reflect"

—Mark Twain

"Some even believe we are part of a secret cabal working against the best interests of the United states, characterizing my family and me as "internationalists" and of conspiring with others around the world to build a more integrated global political and economic structure— one world, if you will.
If that's the charge, then I stand guilty, and I am proud of it."

—David Rockefeller

"If voting made any difference they wouldn't let us do it"

—Mark Twain

ADDENDUM C

A New Financial Model

Money is the lifeblood of all economies and businesses. The world of finance is all about supplying much-needed money to people, businesses, and national economies. Financing (supplying money) occurs as a by-product of banks buying assets—debt and ownership.

Banks borrow new first-tier money from the central bank when and as needed to buy assets from persons, businesses, and nations. The two types of assets that banks purchase are equities (ownership) and bonds (debt), and this comprises financing by banks.

If a bank borrows $1 billion from the central bank, a bank can buy up to $19 billion of assets (bonds or equities). In the process of buying $19 billion of assets with only $1 billion of new government money, a bank is able to create $19 billion of new deposits (new second-tier money).

This new second-tier money goes to the people, businesses, or nations selling their assets, and not to the banks buying the assets. However, ownership of the assets purchased with new bank created second-tier money—does go to the banks.

As assets appreciate in value above their initial sale price, bankers can move asset ownership away from their banks, and over to themselves.

It is relatively easy for anyone to see that there is something fundamentally wrong and unfair about the existing financial system. The present system essentially just gives bankers a license to print new money for themselves as they buy assets.

I propose a new financial system that can ensure that people, businesses, and nations have the money they need to grow, conduct business, and thrive, and it will be legal, fair, and sustainable.

When governments started making new money (via central banks), it was a critical mistake. An even bigger mistake was permitting new government money to be deposited in nongovernment banks.

And then permit nongovernment banks to reuse and multiply that new government money twenty times over, thereby effectively making their own new money in the process. And then allow bankers to use that new (bank-made) money to buy companies and other assets, in a de facto *private* and *exclusive* process.

When governments started making new money, they should have also created a government bank to hold that new government money exclusively. Old money can go on deposit in government banks, but not government money on deposit in nongovernment banks.

Of course when governments started making new money, they did create a new government bank, called the central bank, but only to let bankers alone have accounts there. Only to let bankers alone have exclusive access to new government money via overnight lending with the central bank and also with quantitative easing (QE). Only to let bankers alone be the first to buy IPO companies as they are sold.

People and businesses would have found better lending rates with government banks. Only government banks would then have the ability to make new money. New money created by our government does not belong to any one person, or group of persons—it belongs to everyone.

Because new government money belongs to everyone, this makes possible zero-interest loans and mortgages. All the world's ancient religions have said that zero-interest loans and mortgages were possible and even necessary. All the world's ancient traditions have said that the charging of usury (interest) on borrowed money is a serious violation.

With much better lending rates (zero interest charges), over time only government banks would remain. Now we have a situation where only government money remains, and most of it is in nongovernment banks. This is all backwards and inside out, no wonder the world is such a mess for so many—but so great for so few.

The correct way is for government banks to purchase IPO companies with government money. Through our governments, we would then all own those companies.

This is fitting because government money belongs to our government, and not only to a few bankers. The central bank can then disperse all the earnings; from all the companies it owns, to everyone in society as explained in "The Big If" chapter previously.

Capital Flight

State owned banks would also solve the problem of *capital flight* facing many nations. Often when a nation tries to go with a more "social" approach, money is then sent out of the nation to be invested elsewhere.

Many financiers do not like to have money in places where there are some things it cannot buy, such as other banks and oil companies. Capital flight has effectively destroyed the economies of many nations whose government was only trying to do the right thing for its people.

However, if a nation only has one government bank, the central bank, then no government money will go out of the nation and wreak havoc with the economy. Private investors can still move their own personal money out, only not our government money out as well.

"This crippling of individuals I consider the worst evil of capitalism. Our whole educational system suffers from this evil. An exaggerated competitive attitude is inculcated into the student, who is trained to worship acquisitive success as a preparation for his future career.

I am convinced there is only one way to eliminate these grave evils, namely through the establishment of a socialist economy, accompanied by an educational system which would be orientated toward social goals."

—Albert Einstein.

It ain't what you don't know that gets you into trouble. It's what you know for sure that just ain't so.

—Mark Twain

ADDENDUM D

Ownership of Natural Resources

Suppose we lived in a Native American community situated along the Colorado River, near where the Hoover Dam is today. It is known that before the Hoover Dam was built, this area was frequented by extremely intense and dangerous flash floods.

For that reason, tribes did not live along the riverbank. Instead, they lived a few hundred meters up and away from the river. They used the river water for drinking, cooking, and farming. Some people were in the business of transporting water up to the village.

It takes roughly thirty minutes on horseback to travel to the riverbank, fill thirty gallons of water into five-gallon skins, and travel back up to the village. Once a man did this, those thirty gallons of river water became his to sell.

He could try to charge more than one minute per gallon for his water, but if he did, there was nothing to stop you or anyone from just going to the river and getting your own water—at a cost of one minute per gallon.

What follows below did not happen with the Native Americans living along the Colorado River, but it did happen almost everywhere else.

The people in the business of supplying water up to the village make a deal with the village chief. If the chief sells them the rights to the river, and them alone, the water suppliers will support the chief with campaign contributions—kickback money.

Now the water suppliers own the rights to the river reaching one hour on horseback. Now the water suppliers can charge up to five minutes per gallon of water, and everyone will have to pay that high price, or travel one hour upstream to get water for themselves. Otherwise, they would be arrested after a court injunction.

The people of the village are not free anymore to just go get their own water. Corrupt ownership laws block everyone but the owners of the river from taking river water freely.

The owners of the river can charge up to five minutes per gallon. They pay someone one minute per gallon to do the actual work of getting water up to the village. Give one minute a gallon to the chief to keep him in power. And keep three minutes a gallon for themselves. They would get rich and never have to work again. Therefore, this represents a form of slavery.

Now imagine it is a lake instead of a river. And instead of water, it is a lake of oil or ore; or something that we all use, need, and depend on. Some might ask, how it is possible to pay for water in terms of hours, minutes, or units of time.

Time is Money

The ancient money of that time and area was grain and bean seeds. For the local soil and weather conditions it would be well known to all that a certain average quantity of farming time, produced a specific amount of wheat, corn, or whatever grain or bean seeds.

Seeds were slightly salted to chemically block them from germinating—even if they got a little wet at times. After planting them, a little rain would wash away the little salt, and the seeds would sprout and grow. Seeds lasted essentially forever in *seed banks*. Even thousands of years later, they would still germinate and grow.

In that time, there were no airbuses or trucks to transport produce to far distances. It would take weeks just to travel a few hundred kilometers. So only a few delicacies that did not grow locally would be imported. Everyone knew precisely how much farming time was represented by a specific quantity of some grain or bean seeds.

By paying with a specific quantity of certain seeds, they were in effect paying in units of time. This currency was impossible to counterfeit, except through actual work time. And everyone could make new money for themselves, and not only bankers.

Actually, then it was impossible for bankers to make new money for themselves because that would require actual work time. Furthermore, that type of money had real intrinsic value. People need to eat to live, and beans and grains are an important part of a healthy diet. The value of gold and dollar bills is completely arbitrary, contrived, and artificial; they have no innate or intrinsic value. Have you ever eaten dollar-bill soup?

The Native Americans regarded land as a natural resource, in the same way they regarded their rivers and lakes. They could not be privately owned by anyone—except for what one personally needed to live and grow crops on.

If a family found land that was not already in use, it became their land by simply using it—and only by using it. It would remain their land via its continued use. There were no papers or deeds to confer title or ownership.

With an ox and plow, a family could work only so many acres of land. They only needed that much land to support their family. This created a natural limit on how much land one family could own.

Moreover, the ancients believed that raising livestock for food consumption was a violation of *natural law*. They got their dietary protein from garbanzo and other beans and grains. Skins and meats were sometimes used—but only from hunting, and only enough for what they needed to make medicines and skins.

There was no claiming of thousands of hectares of land to farm livestock. Only the amount of land needed to support a family was allowed.

In Europe and other parts of the world, families would lay claim to thousands of hectares. Others worked the land—but only to give away most of their earnings to the landowner.

Land was won over not by proper use or natural need, but by force. This reminds me of a little story. A traveler was driving around Europe and got a little lost. This was in a time before GPS and smartphones. He noticed a sign on the side of the road: "Private Property—Do Not Enter." The sign had fallen over and in the traveler's mind it was not clear which side the sign referred to.

Fifteen minutes later, he was flanked on both sides by SUVs with armed men. The landowner wanted to see who had ventured on to his land without a proper invite. The land was magnificent and stretched from horizon to horizon and beyond all the way to the sea.

The traveler said, "How did this land come to be yours?"

The landowner said, "It's been in my family for many hundreds of years."

"Yes, but how did it come to be your family's so long ago?"

"We won it in battle."

The traveler said, "Well, okay then, if that's all it takes—off with your coat, and let's have a go at it for the land."

The landlord was not amused and replied, "I don't get into fights. I have my men to fight for me."

The traveler turned to his men and said, "Why would you fight me? I have nothing to lose but my pride. And who wants my pride? He, on the other hand, is the one with all your land."

How strange. It was enough land to feed and house a thousand families, but owned by only this one family and for hundreds of years. Obviously, this family has a very high sense of self-worth, but at everyone else's expense. At least things are improving.

In ancient Egypt, when aristocracy passed away,

they would bury hundreds of slaves away with the deceased. Many time the slaves were still alive when they were buried. This was so that the deceased would have hundreds of slaves ready to wait on them hand and foot in the afterlife. This is megalomania at its worst. We thought we had it bad with Hitler and Mussolini. Yes, things are definitely looking up.

Self-confidence and self-love are important traits to have. And without them, we cannot do anything in life—not even get of bed. The more confidence we have the better. But when do confidence and self-love become arrogance and conceit, avarice and lust?

When with confidence we would take from others what belongs to others? When with love we would deny to others, what we would take for ourselves. When consideration for others and the environment is lost to the small self. Far away from our higher self and the angels of our better nature.

"Everybody is a genius. But if you judge a fish by its ability to climb a tree, it will live its whole life believing that it is stupid".

—Albert Einstein

"I am opposing a social order in which it is possible for one man who does absolute nothing that is useful, to amass a fortune of hundreds of million of dollars, while millions of men and women who work all the days of their lives secure barely enough for a wretched existence."

—Eugene v. Debs

"It's easier to fool people than to convince them that they have been fooled"

—Mark Twain

ADDENDUM E

The Wealth of Nations

Many nations measure their wealth is in terms of how much American dollar reserves they have in their central bank. Colombia is an example that explains the wealth of nations.

Colombian companies need to import many factors of production, such as steel, machines, oil, and so on. However, to buy things abroad, all nations and businesses must pay for goods and services with American dollars. Colombian money only has value in Colombia, Costa Rican money only has value in Costa Rica and so on.

American money is valued everywhere. American money can be changed into any local currency at any bank anywhere in the world. In fact, American money is so universally honored that often travelers do not need to change their American money to the local currency. Instead, we can just use American dollars at point of sale in place of the local currency.

I know what all you drug lords are thinking: *but the last time I was in Serbia, I was able to change my Colombian money into Serbian money at most Serbian banks.* Banks in many nations can change Colombian money to the local currency—but by way of a very different process.

The Serbian bank first changes the Colombian money to American dollars via the central bank of Colombia. And that is only possible, if the central bank of Colombia has American dollar reserves to give in exchange for its Colombian money.

This is usually done through a 3rd party clearing bank in the United States. But ultimately, all clearing banks change their Colombian pesos to American dollars, via the Central bank of Colombia.

The American dollars acquired from this conversion are then changed to Serbian money, via the central bank of Serbia. The central bank of Serbia is able to change American dollars directly into Serbian money.

The American to Serbian money conversion is based solely on the universally recognized value of American money globally. On that basis, the Serbian central bank will accept American dollars directly as a form of payment in exchange for Serbian money. And then keep the American dollars gained from this exchange (sale of Serbian money) on reserve at the Serbian central bank.

Globally, all central banks keep reserves of American dollars, but they do not keep reserves of Colombian pesos. The Serbian central bank will not accept Colombian money directly as a form of final payment in exchange for Serbian money. This is because Colombian money is only honored in Colombia, but Serbia is in Serbia.

Whereas, American dollars have value globally. American dollars are used and honored globally to transact payments both locally and internationally. For all nations, American dollars are the common currency of exchange.

The history of how American money became so universally used and valued will be discussed shortly. It is a direct consequence of the Second World War, which in turn gave rise to the creation of the World Bank.

To summarize: if it is American money in Serbia, then the Serbian central bank will accept american money directly as a form of payment in exchange for Serbian money, without the need to ultimately change American money into American money, by referring to America's central bank (a.k.a. the Fed).

All central banks will accept American money directly as a form of final payment in exchange for their local host currency. This is because not only is American money good in Serbia—it is good everywhere.

Ultimately this means, if Colombian companies and people want to buy products from other nations, they cannot just pay for those imports with Colombian money directly. Instead, they must pay with American dollars.

However, Colombian companies and people can only change their Colombian money to American dollars at some bank. And all banks change Colombian money to American dollars from dollar reserves ultimately held at Colombia's central bank. At an exchange rate set by Colombia's central bank.

If Colombia's central bank is out of American money— with little or no American money reserves—Colombian money becomes worthless—because there is no other way for Colombian companies or people to change their Colombian money into American money.

Therefore, if Colombia's central bank runs out of American dollar reserves, whatever Colombia does not produce locally cannot be purchased. This includes cars, phones, oil, steel, machines, and so much more. And even numerous things produced locally often contain many materials that come from abroad, and therefore cannot be produced without American money.

Without American money reserves, the value of Colombian money would fall to nothing on the world stage. Colombia, its companies and people, would be penniless and unable to buy anything from other nations and even many things produced locally.

That is why most nations measure their wealth in terms of how much American dollar reserves they have in their central bank. And for all nations (other than the USA) American dollar reserves can only come from having a net trade surplus with other nations.

A trade surplus means that a nation is earning more than it is spending. Earning means producing and exporting. Spending means importing and consuming. If we earn more than we spend, then we build up our money reserves.

A trade deficit means that a nation is spending more than it is earning. If we spend more than we earn, then we use up our money reserves, and soon we need to borrow to stay afloat.

If a nation is low on American dollar reserves, then the nation cannot give value to its own national currency, and must then devalue its currency by lowering the exchange rate in relation to the American dollar.

Devaluing the currency slows the rate of burn (loss)

of American dollar reserves—in part by making imports more costly. By making imports more expensive, less imports can be afforded. This slows the rate of drain of American money going out of the nation to buy imports.

Lowering the exchange rate also makes exports more attractive (less expensive) to other nations, thereby increasing the rate of inflow of American dollars to buy that nation's exports.

Most nations carry their debt in terms of American dollars from loans with the IMF or the World Bank. Suppose a nation's debt was ten billion pesos of its own national currency. After a devaluation by a factor of two (cutting currency value in half) a nation would then owe twenty billion pesos and not only ten billion pesos as before.

Everyone of that nation then has to work twice as hard or twice as long to payback their debt in dollars. Everyone also lost half their wealth overnight and took a huge 50 percent pay cut in relation to the rest of the world.

Therefore, the amount of American dollar reserves each nation has, is what gives value to each nation's own currency. The more dollar reserves a nation has, the stronger and more valued its own national currency. For all nations (but the United States), the only way for a nation to have more dollar reserves is from having a trade surplus.

However, the United States does not need to have a trade surplus to have more dollar reserves. Simply because the United States can print more dollars when and as it likes. All other nations can only have more American dollars by earning them, which means producing and selling abroad more than they consume.

This gives the United States an incredibly profound advantage over the rest of the world. This allows the United States to counterfeit money to pay its bills and buy goods abroad, and do so with only minimal inflation. Other nations can also print (counter-fiat) more money, but their money is only good locally.

Costa Rica can also print more pesos, but Costa Rican companies and people cannot use their money (directly) to purchase products outside of Costa Rica. If new money is constrained to a small local region, then the currency is subjected to considerable inflation when more is printed.

When the United States prints a few trillion new dollars from quantitative easing (QE), this new money spreads throughout the whole economy, and eventually gets spent on imports as Americans buy cars, phones, and oil. When the United States prints a few trillion new dollars, there is only minimal inflation because the world is a big place compared to a small nation.

A large portion of new QE money on deposit in American banks can be used to purchase assets globally (as only American money can do). Banks can use and reuse money twenty times over after it is deposited, including new government money, once it is deposited from quantitative easing.

Therefore, global assets purchased by American banks are paid for with counterfeited money. No one had to work to earn that money. The same goes for American assets purchased by American banks. They were purchased with money that was not earned but counterfeited.

The World Bank and International Monetary Fund

The World Bank was created in the last years of the Second World War. Many nations needed food, supplies, and guns in the conflict, but because of the war, they were not able to produce these things for themselves. And for the same reason, they were also not able to pay for them in the short term. The United States created the World Bank so that foreign nations could borrow American dollars to buy food and guns from American producers.

The Second World War greatly invigorated and expanded America's capacity to produce. The United States was too far away from Germany and Japan to be bombed. America became the top supplier of food, tanks, planes, ships, and guns for the world.

The Second World War left the United States the greatest industrial force on earth. It left Europe, Russia, China, and Japan in ruin. China lost twenty million people to that war; second only to Russia that lost twenty-seven million people.

The International Monetary Fund (IMF) was created at the end of the Second World War. In the aftermath of the war, large parts of the world needed to rebuild their nations from the ground up. Cities, bridges, roads, factories, and homes all needed to be rebuilt. However, as a result of the war, only the United States had the industrial capacity to supply the world with the much-needed food, steel, cement, and heavy equipment on a global scale.

The same nations that desperately needed to rebuild, also had no factories or infrastructure left to generate earnings and make payments. Responding to the needs of the time, the United States created the International Monetary Fund (IMF) to loan money to nations needing to rebuild from the war, and then later to developing nations needing to build—taken together that means almost every nation.

When a nation has a printing press to make any amount of new money, then lending money to the whole world becomes a very easy thing to do. It is actually free. There's only the cost of the ink and the paper. This is the history of how American dollars became the global reserve currency used by the world to transact payments both internationally and even locally.

If any nation (other than the United States) has a trade deficit, then that nation's dollar reserves are reduced by that same amount. If any nation (other than the United States) has a trade surplus, then that nation's dollar reserves are increased by that same amount.

The United States started to run a trade deficit in 1974, and over the last forty years has raked up an aggregate deficit of roughly $15 trillion-dollars [11]. That is how much the United States owes the rest of the world. If any nation other than the United States had done the same, then that nation would owe the IMF or the World bank $15 trillion-dollars.

Yet, however much the United States owes the world, that is nothing compared to how much the world owes the United States. There is no dollar amount that can be attached to the stopping of fascism and the alternate future that could have been under Hitler or Japan. The United States was pivotal in deciding the outcome of that epic battle for the world.

Russia can also take much credit for defeating Hitler and stopping fascism, but sadly, whatever credit Russia gained from stopping Hitler, was also lost by starting Hitler. Russia under Stalin was largely responsible for starting the Second World War.

Hitler never would have started his campaign to take Europe had he not first secured an alliance with Russia (through Stalin). The Second World War started just days after Hitler signed a pact with Stalin. A deal that would have carved up postwar Europe. Germany was to get England, France, and a few other places, and Russia would get the rest.

However, after Hitler saw how easy it was to take Europe, he changed the deal. He would keep all of Europe and take Russia as well. If only they had let Hitler in to study art. He really just wanted to be an artist and a painter, not a world conqueror.

It may be that Americans well deserve their entitlements afforded by their global money printer. In the immortal words of Winston Churchill, *"Never was so much owed by so many too so few."*

But Churchill was not only speaking about America's contribution. He was speaking of that generation (from many nations) that stood up to despotism and said with one voice, *over my dead body, it stops here, it stops now.* And for more than seventy million brave allied souls, it would be over their dead bodies. The stopping of a very dark alternate world future was the *"so much"*. They who did the stopping were *"so few"*. And all the future generations to come are the *"so many"*.

Globally, there are only four currencies that can be used directly outside of their respective nations: The United States dollar, British pound, Japanese yen, and the Euro. In practical terms it means that all central banks will accept these four currencies directly as a form of final payment in exchange for their local host currency. This in turn requires that central banks globally receive, and then keep these four currencies as final payment—to then become *reserve currencies*.

Other currencies need to be changed to one of these four *reserve currencies* before they can be changed to the local host currency. And ultimately, this change to a *reserve currency* can only be done through each nation's own central bank. Provided that a nation's central bank has a supply of *reserve currencies* to make the exchange possible. If a nation's central bank is out of *reserve currencies*, then that nation's money becomes worthless, and that nation is officially bankrupt.

The euro is almost as universally valued as the United States dollar and is generally regarded as a pseudo-global currency. However, Greece, Spain, and Portugal cannot just print more euros as they like. They can, however, print more sovereign government bonds and then sell their bonds to the European Central Bank (ECB), which is just the same as printing more euros.

However, EU member nations do not have sovereign control over the ECB and must wait for periods of quantitative easing as decided by the ECB. European Union member states are at the mercy of the ECB as to which nations bonds it will buy, how much, and when. This is what I meant by EU member nations cannot just print more euros as they like.

At present there are twenty-eight EU member states, of which nineteen have embraced the euro as their national currency. The euro is a pseudo-global currency representing 20 percent of global reserves.

Japan also has a pseudo-global currency, the yen, and it is valued (used) mostly in the Asia-Pasific region, and it accounts for 5 percent of global reserves. The United Kingdom also has a pseudo-global currency, the pound sterling, and it also represents 5 percent of global reserves. In contrast, the United States dollar is a true global currency, and it denotes 70 percent of global reserves.

These reserve percentages are not by accident. They are set by the World Bank. The World Bank may have the word "World" in its name, but it is an American institution.

When the United States and the three pseudo-global currency nations are not putting new money into the world economy (from quantitative easing), then total national surpluses must balance out total national deficits.

Similar to the poker game analogy used in the second chapter. For a few nations to be earning X dollars, then the rest must be losing X dollars. On the level of nations, aggregate trade surpluses must balance out aggregate trade deficits.

If half the world's nations have trade surpluses, then mathematically, the other half *must have* deficits. This forces roughly half of the world's nations to take loans from the IMF or the World Bank, and also lower their exchange rates to better compete.

Some years later it might be the other half forced to take loans and lower their exchange rates. Lowering the exchange rate is often a precondition for IMF and World Bank loans. As a result, most nations are forced to fight against each other in this way. And in the process make the US dollar stronger and stronger with each new IMF and World Bank loan.

Except, the United States is 70 percent removed from the fighting. Nineteen EU member states are each 1 percent removed from the fighting. And Japan and the United Kingdom are each 5 percent free from the fight.

Reforms Before Loans

The IMF and World Bank often require "*reforms*" before they will lend money to nations. Reforms means the selling of state-owned assets to the private sector—the uber rich and private bankers.

Assets include state-owned banks, water, electric, utilities, oil, gas, steel, cement, and telephone companies. If it's owned by the state (the people), then it must go, and usually at bargain basement prices. Reforms also include new and modern taxing schemes.

Perhaps it was not taxes and privatization that made America and parts of Europe so wealthy. The IMF says do these reforms and your nation can become affluent like ours. Perhaps it was simply the advantage of having a currency that is valued globally and a printing press. There can be no greater wealth creator than a license to print money that is good everywhere and not just valued locally.

The reforms that the IMF and World Bank have imposed on emerging nations might only make things worse for many developing countries. State-owned natural resources and state-owned essential services may be the way that many emerging nations have learned to cope and survive in a world where they cannot just counterfeit money to pay their bills and buy goods abroad. And besides, some emerging nations might have more social than antisocial temperaments.

This quote comes from the prominent author Naomi Klein, "We are of the opinion that the World Bank loans have unfair conditions attached to them that reflect the interests, financial power, and political doctrines (notably the Washington Consensus) of the World Bank."

Klein says the World Bank's credibility was damaged "when it forced school fees on students in Ghana in exchange for a loan. When it demanded that Tanzania privatize its water system. When it made telecom privatization a condition of loans for rebuilding after Hurricane Mitch.

When it demanded "labor flexibility" (weaker unions and union concessions) in Sri Lanka in the aftermath of the Asian tsunami. When it pushed for eliminating food subsidies in post-invasion Iraq".[5] This list could go on forever. I wonder, would the World Bank force the United States to end social security and food stamps?

Global Currency Woes

The solution to the global currency problem may (or may not) involve granting all nations a representative share of central bank reserves globally, based on each nations share of the global population. However, there is the risk that this may only amplify an even more fundamental underlying flaw in the global financial system.

Now we have a situation where the United States has a global money printer, and Europe and Japan have their tiny little printers. The global economy can still survive with this level of malfeasance. Although, it won't be so pleasant for those nations that don't have printers. But, if we give every nation a money printer, then soon the global economy would fall apart hard.

Assume for a moment that all nations were granted a proportionate share of central bank reserves globally; would outlawing quantitative easing (taking away the printers) for all nations remedy this would be solution?

Even if every nation signed up to such a law, and there was no cheating, then this does not address an even deeper underlying defect in the financial system. And this defect would only then be amplified one hundred and ninety-five times—once for each nation.

Moreover, even if all nations did adhere to a no QE law, there is still the issue of overnight lending with central banks. Central bank lending is just another way of doing QE. So it would be necessary to outlaw both QE and central bank lending by all nations.

Another concern is, how would 196 currencies behave in a global market? There could be resonance effects caused by market feedback loops and fluctuating exchange rates?

There might be a more direct and simple solution to this problem. A simple elegant way to remove all peoples and nations from the fighting, so that we can all prosper and enjoy, in peace, comfort, and ease. Hint: a component of the global currency solution may involve what is discussed in addendum C. The next edition of this book hopes explore these questions more fully.

Unfortunately, I have to say something about gold or some people will think to bring back gold as a solution. Down through the ages, gold as a currency was forced on society by the gold rich "nobles" of Asia and Europe.

Gold is very scarce, and we cannot just make more gold with a little work time in a field. You could go on looking for lifetimes and still not find any gold. Ergo, if you are one of those few people with a surplus of gold, and you also made it illegal to buy land and other big ticket items—unless those items are purchased using gold—then people are going to have to borrow your gold to buy those big items. With substantial interest fees of course.

When the ancient money was grain and bean seeds, we could just grow more money as we needed. However, if buying must be done in gold, and only a few people have a surplus of gold, and we cannot just grow more gold, then everyone will have to borrow gold from the few who have too much of it. With considerable interest fees. People and their genius ways of turning other people into their slaves.

The relationship between time worked—for gold produced—is nebulous, and time is money. Gold is completely wrong as a medium of exchange. That is unless, you want to enslave most of society to debt, and then gold it is the perfect choice for money.

In parts of China, India, and Asia, it is still in some law books from past times, in order to buy land and some other big items, such as other people (slaves) or a wife, then the purchase must be done in gold.

Now days that is not so much a problem. Gold is not nearly as scarce as it once was; not since now we can just walk into any bank and buy gold. But back in the day, we could not just buy gold, because gold was the money. It would mean using gold to buy gold. Would you buy a dollar with a dollar? Maybe, but first you would need a dollar.

The Nobles did not pay for food with gold. Food was the rent (money) paid by the *fiefs* of the field to the *nobles*—and the nobles owned all the land. Until recently, gold was very scarce to the common man. For that reason, most common folk used grain and bean seeds as the pseudo-money of that time.

The global currency problem is partly why half the world is somehow living on only a dollar a day. And also why the United States is doing so well, even in spite of its market, banking, and monetary systems. And in spite of its massive trade deficit that's been going on for more than forty years.

Take away America's printers (quantitative easing, central bank lending, and the money multiplier effect) and take away America's global currency (the dollar), and put the United States on equal footing with other nations, and the United States would fold like a nun in a game of strip poker without her rosary. And most likely bring the rest of the world down with it! I believe this would unleash too much anarchy for the world to handle.

If that did happen, then the United States would discover the value and need of having more shared ownership of natural resources and essential services.

And then the few at the top could not afford the luxury of being so greedy at everyone else's expense.

Then China might be the new overlord nation; forcing privatization on the United States and the rest of the world. So that Chinese financiers can swoop in and buy up American resources on the cheap, with counterfeited money that no one had to work for to earn.

The only reason the United States is doing to so well, and America's affluent can afford to live so large, is because of $22 trillion dollars of public debt, and another $15 trillion dollars that was essentially gifted to America's owner stockholders from forty years of trade deficits [11]. And this is not even counting private and corporate debt. Takeaway the $15 trillion that was gifted to America by the rest of the world, and you would see a big change in living standards of America's owner financiers.

Unfortunately, at this time more cannot be said of the global currency solution. However, until we have a solution, we need to ask ourselves an important question. Has the United States been a good custodian of its printer power in the family of nations?

For more than seventy years the United States has had atomic weapons, and in that time the U.S. has not used them once in aggression. Twice, is the number of times that the United States has used atomic weapons in aggression. On civilian population centers no less—not on military targets. The only country on earth to ever do such a thing.

As soon as the United States had successfully tested its first atomic bomb, it could have pulled all servicemen out of harm's way and sent everybody home. A short time later, an open letter stamped and addressed to Japan could have expressed the situation.

The A-bomb's overwhelming destructive power could have been demonstrated on an uninhabited location. Similar to what was done at the Bikini Atoll in 1946. Google "Baker Atom Bomb at Bikini Atoll 1946"—see it on YouTube [7].

If that failed to convince the Japanese government that surrender was in their best interest, then there was always the option of dropping A-bombs on military targets. At least then some of the blood would be on Japanese hands, because then they would have shared in the decision and could have stopped it themselves.

We could talk about the Vietnam war. The United States intervened in another nation's war on the other side of the world. All because a majority of the Vietnamese people wanted the very same thing that Americans themselves had already done (almost).

The Vietnamese people wanted a more social than anti-social government. They wanted a government *of the people, by the people, for the people*—just like us. They wanted a nation where the people own their government, and their natural resources, and not only a few at the top through the bribery of government officials. Moreover, that was their decision to make and their right to do.

The Vietnam War (with the United States) lasted more than ten years, killing over a million Vietnamese civilians, over half a million Vietnamese soldiers, and over two hundred thousand American servicemen dead.

Actually, for the Vietnamese people that war lasted more than thirty years. The first twenty years of that war was against the French. Question: what is France and the United States doing in Vietnam?

Imagine if China had intervened in America's revolutionary war, or America's civil war, and now all Americans had to singing God save the Queen, eat crumpets and haggis, play soccer instead of football, and still had to send boatloads of tea and gold to a royal family in Europe. Americans would complain but that was our war and our business. It was not China's place to interfere with our lives and our future.

We could talk about how the United States orchestrated the overthrow of the legitimately elected government of Iran, to install the Shaw of Iran, who then privatized Iran's oil at the bidding of the United States. And we wonder why that part of the world does not trust Americans.

A similar story in Panama, when the United States installed Manuel Noriega as the president; a former CIA operative, international drug lord, and murderer. And when Noriega became so bad that even the CIA could not stomach him any longer, the CIA had to put down their dog.

For what follows and for the remainder of this addendum, is a brief summary of Americas involvement in Latin America. But first, I would like to say something about the sources for what follows.

Sources:

[1] Blum, William. Rogue State: A Guide to the World's Only Superpower. Common Courage Press, 2005.

[2] Blum, William. Killing Hope: US and CIA Interventions Since World War II. Common Courage Press, 2003.

Note that these books were written and published over ten years ago. As a result, they are somewhat dated by now. Sam Smith had the following to say of William Blum's books:

> *"Bill Blum simply tested America by the same standards we use to judge other nations. The result is a bill of wrongs—an especially well documented encyclopedia of malfeasance, mendacity and mayhem that has been hypocritically carried out in the name of democracy by those whose only true love was power."*

Before beginning the litany of wrongs, I would first like to put a little history into context. There seems to be some confusion about what *socialism* is or isn't. *Socialism* refers to an economic system and not a political one. Examples of political systems are *democracy, monarchy, plutocracy, dictatorships* and so on.

Socialism is an economic system where the production and distribution of natural resources are for the benefit of all—and not only for a few at the top. Many nations that attempted so called "*socialism*" were not very democratic about it, and some were even outright brutal dictatorships. China during its *cultural revolution* is a good example of this. As was neighboring Cambodia when China exported its revolution there.

Forcing millions of families out of their homes at gun point, then marching them off to work in the fields, for years on end, and for no payment in return—is not socialism—it is simply slavery!

Murdering tens of millions of innocent people, only because they had a good education or could play a musical instrument—is not socialism—it was monstrous insanity. All this actually happened in the name of socialism.

This gave advanced democracies great concern over so called *"socialism"* and rightly so. To put it into perspective, socialism at that time in world history invoked the same emotional response as radical Islam does with us today.

This very negative view of socialism was a direct result of places like China and Cambodia with their cultural revolution, and Stalin with his brand of "socialism". However, it was not socialism, but somehow called that.

Many failed to notice that among numerous so called *right leaning* governments, they also had their share of brutal dictatorships, but nothing compared to the insanity of what happened in China and Cambodia with their cultural revolution.

Another repugnant aspect of this brand of so called socialism, was the taking away of peoples hard earned property. Whether that property be land or companies— this to is not socialism; it is simply theft.

It all comes down to one thing; how was the money acquired that bought the land or companies. If the money was earned, then whatever it buys was also earned and rightfully belongs to the buyer.

The system presented by this book is a free market system, but some will call it socialism. And the system that we now call a free market, is anything but free. There are numerous extortion costs from various obstacles on many levels.

Among the most damaging of these obstacles, are the ones that put most of the ownership and earnings—of most large companies—in the hands of only a few. When really it was all of us that paid for those companies as they went public.

If this book proposes socialism, then it is socialism by way of a free market economy—not only in name, but in actuality. President Woodrow Wilson had the following to say on the issue of man-made obstacles versus a free market economy. Keep in mind that President Wilson was speaking from his era when he said these words:

"They know that America is not a place of which it can be said, as it used to be, that a man may choose his own calling and pursue it just as far as his abilities enable him to pursue it; because to-day, if he enters certain fields, there are organizations which will use means against him that will prevent his building up a business which they do not want to have built up; organizations that will see to it that the ground is cut from under him, and the markets shut against him. For if he begins to sell to certain retail dealers, to any retail dealers, the monopoly will refuse to sell to those dealers, and those dealers, afraid, will not buy the new man's wares."

—President Woodrow Wilson. The New Freedom, Chapter I: The Old Order Changeth

Before beginning the list of wrongs, I would like to again remind readers of the deep concern that the free world had for socialism at that time in world history. The free world looked to China and Cambodia in shock and horror at their cultural revolution.

The free world did not want a repeat of that bizarre perversion of socialism taking root in other nations, such as in Latin America. Or, maybe I am speaking out of time and place, when I suggest this cause and effect relationship. Perhaps, what happened in Latin America, as expressed by the litany of wrongs (soon to follow), was motivated mostly from a level of greed.

There is one telling fact that speaks to this question of cause and effect. It's a question of which came first (chicken or egg). Much of what happened in the litany of wrongs came before the cultural revolution got underway (1966). America entered the Vietnam war a full two years before the start of the Cultural revolution.

The Indochina wars of Laos, Cambodia and Vietnam started in 1945; a full twenty years before the start of the cultural revolution. These small southeast Asian nations had been colonized (taken over) by France (not China). The Indochina wars began as a resistance movement. The indigenous population was trying to throw off an occupying force of armed and pushy invaders, and it grew into what we now call the Vietnam war.

After twenty long years of fighting against the French and Japanese—Cambodia and Laos had enough fighting. Vietnam (or half of it anyway) was the only one still willing to give push back on this issue. So it then became the Vietnam War, and no more the Indochina wars. If we include Japan in this discussion, then that makes forty-five years of war in that area of the world starting in 1931.

That much war, death and destruction (twenty-five million dead), over that long a period of time (45 years), it tends to drive a people crazy. Hence, the cultural revolution in that part of the world.

If only the Japanese, French, and Americans had gone there armed with suntan lotion and beach toys—instead of guns—the cultural revolution may never have happened.

The leaders of the cultural revolution looked at their own history and that of the world. And they looked at the behavior of people in general. They concluded that all the problems of society and the world, are created by the way people behave when they become too high-falutin.

Their solution was to turn everyone into simple peasant farmers. They believed that if everyone had their own land to grow on, and their own family (and no more high-falutin) that this would bring an end war and poverty. The two most important things to them by that point in time. So important that the means didn't matter in the end.

Now for the Litany of Wrongs.

The Litany of Wrongs

Guatemala 1954:

A CIA-organized coup overthrew the democratically elected and progressive government of Jacobo Arbenz. The United States justified its involvement by claiming that the Soviets had an uncomfortable level of influence over Guatemala, even though the two countries didn't even maintain diplomatic relations.

A more likely reason for United States involvement came from the United Fruit Company, whose land would have been expropriated as part of Arbenz's progressive land reforms. The Arbenz's government had offered United Fruit the declared value of their unused land. The government was not planning to expropriate land that was already in use by any company or persons—only unused land.

The CIA action in Guatemala became the blueprint for CIA interventions across Latin America. The bribery of military officers. Propaganda campaigns against the government. The resurrection of opposition parties and oppositional radio stations. The mass distribution of anti-government leaflets and the anonymous submission of news articles that painted the Arbenz government as communist and corrupt.

The United States also used international political and financial clout to pressure the UN to ignore Arbenz's request for an investigation of the incident. The coup was followed by 40-years of instability and brutality in Guatemala.

British Guiana (currently Guyana) 1953-64:

CIA and British Intelligence funded anti-communist unions in order to strengthen opposition to democratically elected Dr. Cheddi Jagan. When this failed, the Churchill government simply removed him from office due to his socialist leanings.

In 1957, Jagan was re-elected, and in response the United States Information Service launched an anti-communist (anti-Jagan) media campaign.

Despite this, Jagan was re-elected again in 1961, which moved the British government to organize strikes in the unions that they had previously funded. The British government used these strikes as a sign of incompetence on the part of Jagan and changed the constitution to remove him from power.

Cuba 1959-present:

After the Cuban revolution in 1959, the United States did everything in its power to prevent its government from succeeding. The United States performed air raids and even mobilized Cuban exiles to attack Cuba in the infamous CIA-orchestrated Bay of Pigs.

The United States also enacted trade and credit embargos, sabotaged goods destined for Cuba, made multiple assassination attempts on Castro, his brother Raul, and Che Guevara.

Ecuador 1960-63:

The CIA infiltrated the Ecuadorian government, set up news agencies and radio stations, bombed right-wing agencies and churches and blamed the left, all to force democratically elected Velasco Ibarra from office. (See operation Northwoods)

When his replacement, Carlos Arosemara, refused to break relations with Cuba, the CIA-funded military took over the country, outlawed socialism, and cancelled the 1964 elections.

Brazil 1961-64:

After democratically elected Janio da Silva Quadros of the Brazilian Labor Party (PTB) resigned, citing military and United States pressure as the reasons, his successor, Joao Goulart, was overthrown by a United States-supported military coup in 1964.

Critics argue that this is because Goulart promoted social and economic reforms, limited the profits of multinationals, nationalized a subsidiary of United States-owned International Telephone and Telegraph (ITT), and refused to break relations with Cuba and other socialist countries.

He was replaced by two decades of a brutal military regime. There would not be another Labor Party president until the election of Lula da Silva in 2002.

Peru mid-1960's:

The CIA set up military training camps and provided arms to the Peruvian government to combat revolutionary forces.

Dominican Republic 1963-65:

In 1963, Juan Bosch took office as the first democratically elected president of the Dominican Republic since 1924. He was a true liberal and called for land reform, low-rent housing, modest nationalization of business, and restrictions on foreign investment.

Seven months after being elected, the United States allowed a right wing military coup to take over the government. Nineteen months later, a popular revolution broke out which attempted to reinstate Bosch. The United States reacted by sending in troops to stop the Bosch revolutionaries. Meanwhile, the CIA and United States Information Agency (USIA) conducted an intensive propaganda campaign against Bosch.

United States troops stayed in the Dominican Republic until September 1966, when, thanks in part to the anti-Bosch media campaign, Juan Bosch lost the election to Joaquin Balaguer.

Uruguay 1964-1970:

The CIA and the Agency for International Development (AID) set up the Office of Public Safety (OPS) mission in Montevideo to train police in the art of torture in order to suppress rebel activity. The torture and killing was mainly directed at the Tupamaros, revolutionary forces who embarrassed public officials and exposed corporate corruption.

Now that Tabare Vasquez, Uruguay's new left-leaning

president, is in office, many who were once Tupamaro rebels are now holding positions in government. This roster includes Agriculture minister Jose Pepe Mujica and Federal deputy Luis Rosadilla, who previously spent nine years in prison for his rebel activities.

Chile 1964-1973:

After the CIA unsuccessfully prevented Salvador Allende from winning the Chilean presidency by spreading propaganda and funding the opposition, it concentrated its efforts on getting Allende overthrown.

The campaign, which involved bribing officers and spreading misinformation, was eventually successful and the brutal dictator General Augusto Pinochet overthrew Allende in 1973. Allende died during the overthrow and seventeen years of repressive military rule followed.

The recently elected Chilean president, Michelle Bachelet, was herself imprisoned and tortured by Pinochet's regime, as was her father, who died while still in captivity. In her acceptance speech, Bachelet promised to lead with tolerance, saying "because I was the victim of hatred, I have dedicated my life to reverse that hatred and turn it into understanding, tolerance and — why not say it — into love."

Bolivia 1964-75:

In 1952, an armed popular revolt defeated the military, displaced the oligarchy, nationalized the mines, instituted land reform, set up a new government, and reduced the military to an impotent force.

Yet under the training (School of Americas) and financial support of the CIA and Pentagon, the military was built up again and overthrew President Victor Paz in 1964 because of his refusal to support Washington's Cuba policies. This was nothing new for Bolivia, which has experienced the passing of governments more frequently than the passing of years.

In January 2006, as Evo Morales was sworn in as Bolivia's first indigenous president, he predicted a future of indigenous rule, saying, "We are here to say enough of the 500 years of Indian resistance.

From 500 years of resistance, we pass to another 500 years in power." Later that year, Morales sent Bolivian troops to occupy 56 gas installations and demanded all foreign energy-firms sign new contracts giving Bolivia majority ownership and as much as 82% of revenues, which they did.

Argentina 1970's:

While Argentina was receiving worldwide condemnation for their human rights abuses during the "Dirty War" against left-wing dissidents, United States Secretary of State Henry Kissinger was recorded giving the go-ahead to then-Argentine foreign minister Augusto Guzzetti. "We would like you to succeed," said Kissinger of the civil war against the Argentine leftists. From 1975 to 1983, about 30,000 civilians accused of subversion either died or disappeared.

Nicaragua 1978-1990:

When the Sandinistas overthrew the Somoza dictatorship in 1979, the United States was frightened by what they thought could be another Cuba. President Jimmy Carter tried to sabotage the revolution through economic and diplomatic forms, and later Reagan used violence.

For eight years, Nicaragua faced military attacks by the United States funded Contras (Reagan's "freedom fighters). In 1990, the United States interfered in national elections, and the Sandinistas were defeated.

According to Oxfam, the international development organization, Nicaragua under the Sandinistas was "exceptional in the strength of that government's commitment...to improving the condition of the people and encouraging [an] active development process." Now, Nicaragua is one of the poorest nations in the hemisphere, with widespread illiteracy and malnutrition.

Honduras 1980's:

Honduras was basically a colony of the United States during the Contra war in Nicaragua. Thousands of United States troops were housed there and it was used as a supply center and refuge for the Contras. The United States funded the Contras by covertly and illegally selling arms to Iran (known as the Iran-Contra Affair).

Grenada 1979-1983:

A 1979 coup took control of this small island country and attempted to install socialist reforms. The Reagan administration used destabilization tactics and eventually invaded in 1983, resulting in United States as well as Grenadian casualties.

El Salvador 1980-92:

After the United States helped fix an election to repress dissidents in El Salvador, the rebels turned to violence and a civil war ensued. Although the United States claimed to be only involved on an advisory basis 20 United States soldiers were killed in combat missions. The United States spent six billion dollars repressing this popular revolution.

Haiti 1987-94:

After supporting the Duvalier family dictatorship for 30 years and opposing Jean-Bertrand Aristide, the United States claimed to support the elections that returned Aristide to power after he was ousted by a 1991 military coup.

Meanwhile, they warned Aristide that they would only allow him to rule if he implemented free market policies. Aristide did not remain in power for long, however, and in a subsequent interview he attributed his removal from power to his refusal to privatize Haiti's state-owned enterprises.

The 2004 coup was orchestrated by the leaders of the FRAPH, or Haitian Front for Advancement and Progress, a CIA-backed organization that carried out state terror against opponents of the military regime that ruled the country from 1991 to 1994.

Another leader in the armed coup against Aristide was Guy Philippe, a former member of the Haitian military who received training from US Special Forces in Ecuador in the 1990s. After these forces pushed Aristide into exile, the United States stepped in to restore stability in Haiti, now under new rule.

Since Aristide's removal from power, his supporters have been targeted by the UN forces now tasked with "peace keeping," killing many innocents from Haiti's poorest neighborhoods in the process.

Panama 1989:

Just weeks after the fall of the Berlin Wall, the United States invaded Panama, killing thousands and leaving many more wounded and homeless in order to capture Manuel Noriega, a former employee of the CIA and ally of the United States.

Mexico, Peru, and Colombia 1990's to present:

Under the guise of the drug war, the United States has given military aid to these countries. Most of this aid is used to fight rebel forces trying to bring about a more progressive government.

Venezuela:

The recent United States intervention in Venezuela manifests as millions of dollars in contributions to political opponents of leftist President Hugo Chavez. The short-lived 2002 coup d'etat that kidnapped the democratically elected president was orchestrated by groups who had received funding from the United States National Endowment for Democracy (NED).

When the opposition took power, they dissolved all of Venezuela's democratic institutions, including the National Assembly, the Supreme Court, the Constitution, the General Attorney, and the Public Defender's office. Meanwhile, their plan promised a return to free market economic policies. Which is code for private bankers going on a spending spree with our money. The coup only lasted two days before a popular resistance reinstated Chavez.

Conclusion

Okay, the United States may not be the perfect steward of its printer power in the world, but it could be worse (right?). In the illustrious words of Vice President Agnew, *"The United States, for all its faults, is still the greatest nation in the country."* [8]

Interested readers may also refer to the following website www.geopoliticalmonitor.com; where much of the preceding on Americas involvement in Latin America originated.

"Everything which is really great and inspiring is created by the individual who can labor in freedom"

—Albert Einstein

"Everyone can enjoy a life of luxurious leisure if the machine-produced wealth is shared, or most people can end up miserably poor if the machine-owners successfully lobby against wealth redistribution. So far, the trend seems to be toward the second option, with technology driving ever-increasing inequality"

—Stephen Hawking, Famed Physicist. The system proposed by this book is not about wealth redistribution. This book proposes a free market economy. Not just in name, but in actuality.

"The great corporations which we have grown to speak of rather loosely as trusts are the creatures of the State, and the State not only has the right to control them, but it is duty bound to control them wherever the need of such control is shown"

—Theodore Roosevelt, 1902

ADDENDUM F

We All Have Our Little Quirks

Many years ago, I put some of this book online into a political website. Soon after a group of people approached me. They tried to explain that most people need to be controlled, and that the world was not yet ready for the ideas of this book (then a website).

They emphasized that most people were operating from a level of "fear and desire and little else", and were not ready for real freedom. Apparently, everything is set up this way to carry out this level of control. Control takes power, and power requires money. It's a little difficult to articulate in words the problem they talked about. I will attempt to explain this underlying problem with a few examples.

Time Before Trust

A girl became romantically involved with her professor. He was a visiting professor from India. She was so in love that she added him to her bank account—with $150,000 in it. She got pregnant by him. He went back to India with all her money before she gave birth; leaving her to bear and raise a child, broke and alone.

Calm Reflection before Action

A master's degree student was working in a cooperative job placement. Part of his job description was to keep the server and all the computers working smoothly. There were days when the server worked fine, but then others when it did not work at all.

The student was under strict orders not to bring in outside help, even if he was unable to find and fix the problem. One night, at the student's expense, he snuck a technician in to solve the problem.

The technician could not solve the problem on the level of software or settings. So the technician tried something that never occurred to the student. The technician opened the server to check the hardware.

Immediately, both the technician and the student saw the problem. The network interface card was in the wrong position. It was a 16-bit ISA card, in a 32-bit EISA slot, but not in the first row or the "shared slot" as it was called. The shared slot would accept both 16-bit and 32-bit cards.

They put the network card in a correct port, and everything worked fine from then on. In the wrong port, the network never could have worked, but it did work sometimes. This strongly suggests sabotage.

Sadly, without thinking first, the student called his supervisor to tell him what they had just discovered. The supervisor was beyond furious that the student had brought in outside help. He screamed over the phone and threw chairs around in the background.

He was not the least bit interested or surprised that the server had been sabotaged. He was only furious that outside help had been brought in against his explicit and repeated orders.

Never Sign, Until There is No Other Way

A teacher was working in Korea. He was on a city bus when an accident happened and broke his back. He had a compression fracture of the fourth lumbar. His boss offered to act as a translator with the insurance company.

His boss explained that the laws in Korea were different than in Canada. Even though the teacher's injuries were among the most severe possible. His boss said the best the teacher could hope to receive from the insurance company was roughly $15,000 plus medical expenses.

The teacher tried to check this information for himself. He called the Canadian embassy every day and left messages. He sent dozens of e-mails to the embassy and asked for a list of Korean lawyers who were fluent in English. A month passed and still no reply from the embassy. Our tax dollars were hard at work.

The teacher was totally doped on painkillers and muscle relaxants and was in the most extreme pain. He could barely function at all. Finally, the teacher just gave in to the drugs and the pain and signed the settlement with the insurance company.

The day after the settlement, the teacher met his boss at the bank. The boss had him sign bank documents, but everything was in Korean. The teacher didn't know what he was signing. His boss said he was helping the teacher deposit the money from the insurance settlement into the teacher's bank account.

When they reached the bank teller, she placed a large pile of money in front of his boss.

The teacher said, "What is that?"

The boss grinned and said, "My money." As he turned to walk away with the money, the teacher stopped him.

The money from the insurance settlement had already been deposited into the teacher's account the night before. His boss was trying to take that money out for himself. Apparently, whatever deal he made with the insurance company was still not enough.

When the teacher returned to his apartment, his boss was waiting inside. He had a key because the school provided the apartment. He demanded that the teacher go to the bank and return with the money.

The poor teacher was so steeped in being truthful from a lifetime of honesty that it never occurred to him to simply say, "Okay, I will go get the money for you," and return with the police instead. The drugs may have played a part in his lack of judgment. With all the pain and the drugs, he could barely think straight.

When the teacher refused to get the money, his boss picked up a large kitchen knife. Unfortunately, there were no other knives for the teacher to grab. For the first five minutes, his boss just played with him. He lunged at the teacher in mock attacks.

The boss could see that the teacher was terrified, and he utterly enjoyed terrorizing the teacher. The boss's joy turned to rage when he could not scare the teacher enough to get what he wanted. The teacher was more concerned about right and wrong.

The boss lunged at the teacher for real, but the teacher managed to get a grip on the man's wrists. They fell backwards together, landing on the teacher's still broken back, and his boss now on top of him. The boss screamed that he was going to kill the teacher.

The tip of the knife was just an inch or two from the teacher's left eye. Every few seconds, his boss would push the knife with all his strength, trying to make the knife go in. After a few minutes, they were both exhausted.

The teacher realized that soon he would be too tired to keep the knife out. He moved his right hand from the attacker's wrist and over to the far end of the blade. This gave the teacher enough leverage to twist the knife back, and pry it out from his boss's hands.

When the teacher had the knife, his boss suddenly behaved better.

In shock and disbelief, the teacher gasped, "John, you just tried to kill me."

The boss answered, "I cannot help it. Money makes me crazy. Hey, we all have our little quirks."

Perhaps the boss could not stand the thought of someone getting a windfall of insurance money. Instead, he tricked and cheated the teacher out of a few hundred thousand dollars. By his own admission, he was crazy.

The next day, the boss returned with two men and two police officers. John explained that someone had broken into his apartment and attacked him. He said the attacker was now living in his apartment, and the police believed him.

With a smile of satisfaction, John said, "The police think these two men are my brothers, but really they are just two friends I hired for this occasion."

The police were just a few feet away, but they didn't speak English.

John explained that in his nation "there was a matter of family honor". That his brother would be allowed to defend his family's honor. The police went out of the apartment to leave the teacher alone with one of the fake brothers.

The fake brother got into a fighting position and said, "I am black belt in taekwondo."

The teacher said, "I can run one hundred meters in six seconds!"

He tried to explain to the black belt that he still had a broken back, but the man didn't care.

As the black belt started to bear down on him, the teacher let out a bloodcurdling scream. The police ran back into the apartment just in time to save him from the black belt. There was nowhere to run, and he still had a broken back.

Conclusion

There might be some truth to the concern that people need to be controlled. Otherwise, some people can be downright dangerous. Others can be heroic, awesome, and fun to be with.

I didn't need to use these examples to prove my point. I could have used the Holocaust, fascism, operation Northwoods, the Crucifixion of Jesus and of His apostles.

Actually, not all of the apostles were crucified. A few were deep-fried and a few others were barbequed. This list could go on forever.

There is a group that says they have a solution to this problem. A knowledge that can make any person, no matter how awful—impeccably good and clear. However, there's one small problem with the group's theory.

In the preceding examples, all the culprits were from that group. For twenty years or more, and they were also teachers of this knowledge. The boss who ordered the student not to bring in outside help, and the Korean boss who tried to kill the teacher, and his two fake brothers were all from that same group.

The professor from India who ran off with all the student's money after getting her pregnant was also from that group. So much for their knowledge being able to create *ideal behavior* and *spontaneous right action*. So, there is the rhetoric, and then there is the reality.

Pure Stupidity

I felt something hit my face during group meditation. I opened my eyes and saw a pair of panties in my lap. I looked up and my friend said, "They are your wife's panties. She forgot them last night."

There were more than a dozen meditators in the room, and many of them were teachers of this meditation. Everyone overheard this exchange, but not one person there thought ill of it. A few even laughed. Meanwhile, I was devastated to the very core of my being to find out that my wife was cheating on me with a friend I had known for years—and my brothers of the same tradition of knowledge behaved that way.

Those people are supposed to bring ideal behavior to the world through pure knowledge. It's hard to imagine, but I suppose stranger things have happened. When you ask this group about that kind of aberrant behavior, they would say, *"Well, you must have deserved it. That was your karma."* Their guiding philosophy on this comes right from the top.

The founder of this group said, *"Nothing ever happens to anyone that they didn't deserve."* By that logic, I could have punched him in the nose, just for having relayed that pearl of wisdom from the founder. I could have said, *"Hey, I didn't do anything wrong. For that to have happened, you must have deserved it—that was your karma."*

Imagine if a man murders your wife and family. As the judge lets him off with a stern warning, he turns to you and says, *"Well, you must have deserved it."* If a lady is injured on the side of the road, do we stop to help her—or just keep on walking past because she must have deserved it?

We all need to feel that we are protected by laws. We all need to feel that others cannot just do whatever they want to us, especially when they want to hurt us. The people who approached me to explain that people were not ready for real freedom were from this same group. I can understand why they felt that way. I hold back from identifying this group by name, because they're most likely correct.

Still, I think it's a dangerous way to deal with crime and criminals. The only thing that holds many criminals back from doing horrible things is fear of punishment. It is a slippery slope.

However, fear of punishment will only hold back some crime—and only for a while. Desire and anger can build up to a point where they overshadow our fears. If desire cannot be fulfilled, it sublimates into anger.

The only way to stop crime is to provide *everyone* with a legitimate way to *easily* fulfill all our desires and aspirations in life. That is why I present the system of this book.

Jesus said if someone asks you to walk one mile with him, then walk two. This is the origin of the expression *"go the extra mile."* Really, it is an instruction for how to put an end to crime and war. It might be a while before we all wake up to that level of understanding.

Jesus may be the best answer we have to this people problem. His timeless and impeccable example is set like a jewel in truth, and held firm in forgiveness, compassion, and love. He shines as a beacon of hope for all time and all humanity.

If this book is blocked, it will only be because not enough people have the necessary level of maturity to distinguish between right and wrong, pure and impure. They need to be controlled, and control requires power—and power takes money. Everything may need to stay as is for the time being.

However, it is promised that one day we will *"beat our swords into plowshares."* So we are destined to grow up. He will return and guide us home safely. However, until we grow up, there is only a chance that He will be crucified all over again. Hence, His delayed return.

Scriptures say that when He returns, He will *"bear the mark of the cross."* I believe this means physical scars from having been nailed to a cross. However, we need to stay open and flexible on this point.

The cross may denote something more meaningful. The cross may refer to some horrible ordeal that we must all go through at some point in our lives. We all have a cross to bear and to bear our crosses well.

Like the song says, *"What if God was one of us ... just a stranger on the bus, trying to make his way home—like us."*

For some, their ordeals come early in life. If we can survive our ordeals with dignity, this marks or imparts our souls with that same dignity. A dignity that matures our minds and hearts, and even deeper still. This is the mark of the cross. An ordeal is a rite of passage place deeper within.

Ordeal Examples

The examples are as endless and varied as life: The early death of a son or daughter. The loss of a mother, father, wife, husband, or a dear loved one. The loss of a job, poverty, homelessness, sickness, and disease. The plight we see happening every day to tens of millions of families in Syria, Iraq, and all over the world. Half the world somehow living on a dollar a day.

We cannot all sit in the same seat on the bus. Some get the sickness seat, and others get poverty or loss of loved ones. All the various permutations and combinations of these create the many seats on the bus.

The ultimate ordeal was forty days and nights alone

with Satan in the desert. After that, then even being nailed to a cross and dying an incredibly slow, cruel, and painful death would seem like a walk in the park.

The global debt crisis is really a crisis of morality. A moral crisis is really just a spiritual crisis in disguise. Therefore, any solution to the debt crisis must also have a spiritual component. Understanding this will give people hope and inspiration.

The greedy financiers and corrupt politicians are not the root of the problem. We are the root of the problem. Too many of us lack enough maturity, heart, and moral sense to be able to discern the good from the corrupt. We continue to elect corrupt people with precious little true spirituality and goodness.

Since we live in a democracy, we have only ourselves to blame. We must stop electing people because they say the things we like to hear. Telling us how great we must be, that we are from the greatest nation, and that we are the greatest people is called *pandering*. They appeal to our vanity and egos.

Instead, choose a person with a good moral compass, a clear sense of forward direction, and a detailed map for how to lead us to a better, easier, fuller life with a more secure future.

Good luck to all.

"America will never be destroyed from the outside. If we falter and lose our freedoms, it will be because we destroyed ourselves." [9]

—Abraham Lincoln

"Nearly all men can stand adversity, but if you want to test a man's character, give him power."

—Abraham Lincoln

"Shall we expect some transatlantic military giant to step the ocean and crush us with a blow? Never!

All the armies of Europe, Asia, and Africa combined, with all the treasure of the earth in their military chest, and with a Bonaparte for a commander, could not by force take a drink from the Ohio or make a track on the Blue Ridge in a trial of a thousand years.

At what point then is the approach of danger to be expected? I answer. If it ever reach us, [danger] it must spring up amongst us; it cannot come from abroad. If destruction be our lot, we must ourselves be its author and finisher. As a nation of freemen, we must live through all time, or die by suicide."

—Abraham Lincoln in his Lyceum Address, Springfield, Illinois on January 27, 1838

Almost all Americans know the Gettysburg address—some by heart even. But there may be other peoples from other nations who also need to hear these words—some for the first time.

"Four score and seven years ago our fathers brought forth upon this continent a new nation, conceived in Liberty, and dedicated to the proposition that all men are created equal.

Now we are engaged in a great civil war, testing whether that nation, or any nation so conceived, and so dedicated, can long endure. We are met on a great battle-field of that war. We have come to dedicate a portion of that field, as a final resting-place for those who here gave their lives that the nation might live. It is altogether fitting and proper that we should do this.

But, in a larger sense, we cannot dedicate, we cannot consecrate – we cannot hallow – this ground. The brave men, living and dead, who struggled here, have consecrated it far above our poor power to add or detract.

The world will little note, nor long remember what we say here, but it can never forget what they did here. It is for us, the living rather, to be dedicated here to the unfinished work which they who fought here, have, thus far, so nobly advanced.

It is rather for us to be here dedicated to the great task remaining before us – that from these honored dead, we take increased devotion to that cause for which, they here gave the last full measure of devotion.

That we here highly resolve that these dead shall not have died in vain – that this nation, under God, shall have a new birth of freedom – and that a government of the people, by the people, for the people, shall not perish from the earth."

—Abraham Lincoln at Gettysburg, November 19, 1863

Thank god we had Lincoln when we did. When will we ever see the likes of him again?

John F Kennedy. The President addresses the Press.
Waldorf-Astoria Hotel, New York City
April 27, 1961

"In 1851 the New Your Herald Tribune under the sponsorship and publishing of Horace Greeley, employed as its London correspondent an obscure journalist by the name of Karl Marx.

We are told that foreign correspondent Marx, stone broke, and with a family ill and undernourished, constantly appealed to Greeley and managing editor Charles Dana for an increase in his munificent salary of $5 per monthly installment. A salary which he and Engels ungratefully labelled as the "lousiest petty bourgeois cheating."

But when all his financial appeals were refused, Marx looked around for other means of livelihood and fame. Eventually terminating his relationship with the Tribune and devoting his talents full time to the cause that would bequeath to the world the seeds of Leninism, Stalinism, revolution and the cold war.

If only this capitalistic New Your Newspaper had treated him more kindly. If only Marx had remained a foreign correspondent, history might have been different. I hope that all publishers will bear this lesson in mind, the next time they receive a poverty stricken appeal for a small increase in the expense account from an obscure newspaper man."

NOTES

1   Admiral Mike Mullen, May 10, 2012, Chairman of the
Joint Chiefs.
2   This quote was really a paraphrase originally by Charles
Binderup 19 March 1937 in the House of Representatives
(Congressional Record—House 81:2528). Binderup
was paraphrasing Henry Ford when he said [and this
is directly from the congressional record. As seen
with my own eyes. Congressional records have been
digitized and are available online], Binderup said while
congress was in session, *"It was Henry Ford who said in
substance this: 'It is perhaps well enough that the people
of the nation do not know or understand our banking and
monetary system, for if they did, I believe there would be
a revolution before tomorrow morning'"*.
3   Abraham Lincoln to Colonel William F. Elkins, Nov. 21,
1864. There is some controversy about whether or not
Lincoln said this. It easy to see why the corporate elite
would want this quote gone from the books. It started
showing up in books like Emanuel Hertz's Abraham
Lincoln: A New Portrait (1931) and also The Lincoln
Encyclopedia by Archer H. Shaw (1950).

It would be easy to lay this controversy to rest, if only the original letter could be located. This artifact may have been purchased and subsequently destroyed.

Most attempts to discredit the authenticity of this quote are online. The only proof offered is the subjective sense that it does not sound like something Lincoln would have said. However, that depends on the listener. To me, it does sound like something he would have said. Until we have real proof that Lincoln did not say this, I will leave this quote in, with this note attached. Thank you.

4   Abraham Lincoln to Colonel William F. Elkins, Nov. 21, 1864. There is some controversy about whether or not Lincoln said this. It easy to see why the corporate elite would want this quote gone from the books. It started showing up in books like Emanuel Hertz's Abraham Lincoln: A New Portrait (1931) and also The Lincoln Encyclopedia by Archer H. Shaw (1950).

It would be easy to lay this controversy to rest, if only the original letter could be located. This artifact may have been purchased and subsequently destroyed.

All attempts to discredit the authenticity of this quote are online. The only proof offered is the subjective sense that it does not sound like something Lincoln would say. However, that depends on the reader. To me, it does sound like something Lincoln would have said. Until real proof is found that Lincoln did not say this quote, I will leave this quote in, with this note attached. Thank you.

5   This exact quotation has not been found in the writings of Thomas Jefferson. It may be a mistaken amalgamation of a real Jefferson quotation. Fifty years after Jefferson's declaration of independence, and one year before his

death. Jefferson wrote in a letter to William Branch Giles,

"vast accession of strength from their younger recruits, who having nothing in them of the feelings or principles of '76 [year of the declaration of independence] *now look to a single and splendid government of an Aristocracy, founded on banking institutions and monied in corporations, under the guise and cloak of their favored branches of manufactures, commerce, and navigation, riding and ruling over the plundered ploughman and beggared yeomanry."*

[Yeomanry refers to a small military unit comprised of Yeomen. Yeomen are people who usually work in the fields as farmers.]

Giles subsequently comments that *"he [Jefferson] warned that lending institutions and monied incorporations would be the end of democracy and the defeat of the American revolution.".*

6   Klein, Naomi (26 April 2007). "The World Bank has the perfect standard bearer". The Guardian. Retrieved 12 May 2013.

7   https://www.youtube.com/watch?v=5nWFx-zmI0k. "Baker Atom Bomb at Bikini Atoll 1946"

8   Vidal, Gore (December 21, 2000). "Democratic Vistas". The Nation. Retrieved on January 31, 2009

9   Although it is widely held that Lincoln said this, it has yet to be substantiated. It may be a condensed version of his Lyceum Address, Springfield, Illinois on January 27, 1838

10 Actually, there would still be some nominal taxes. Table 1 below shows labor statistics for Canada (from the 2006 census). For that time frame there were roughly

seventeen million people working fulltime in Canada, of which one million worked in essential services.

Table 1: Essential Services

Specialist Physicians	24,505
General Practitioners and Family Physicians	41,870
Nurse Supervisors and Registered Nurses	249,020
Medical support staff	53,380
Police and Fire Fighters	86,430
Secondary and Elementary School Teachers	433,425
Highway, Street, and Bridge construction	57,452
Military (actual soldiers and maintenance crews)	65,450
Total:	1,011,082

One million essential service personnel represents 6 percent of the total full-time work force of seventeen million people (Canada 2006). Hence, a 6 percent income tax applied to everyone would provide enough money to pay the salaries of the 1 million public sector workers. This 6 percent tax could also be implemented as a 3 percent income tax, plus a 3 percent sales tax.

Some analysts might question that doctors and police are paid much more than the average. Note that a corresponding percentage of the private sector also earns much more than the average. A 6 percent tax applied to those higher earners, pays for the higher earners of the public sector.

Some readers might ask, *but why are we paying so much more in taxes than just 6 percent*? That's because the total number of people working in all levels of government, directly and indirectly, comes to almost 3 million (Canada 2006)—doing what exactly I have no idea.

11 A cumulative U.S. trade deficit over a forty-year span and adjusted for inflation to 2016 dollars comes to $15 trillion dollars. From 1975-1985 the trade deficit was averaging $100 million dollars a year. However, forty years ago money was worth five to ten times more than what it's worth now. Over the last twenty years the deficit has averaged roughly $500 million dollars a year.

12 Housing lots can be practically free. This can be done without sacrificing any of the many benefits that comes from having good city planning. The city becomes responsible for maintaining a ready supply of vacant housing lots. Everyone is given a housing lot for free when they turn sixteen. A birthday present from everyone to everyone, if you will. A buffer zone of 5 to 10-kilometer is maintained between the city limits and working farmland.

Farmland is leased for free for the lifetime of the farmer. The government is responsible for maintaining a ready supply of high quality farmland for any would be farmer that asks for it. On occasion the government may need to pay for land (to maintain said land supplies), this expense is passed on to everyone equally as a tax. Once working farmland falls within the buffer zone, then this farmland is retired—as the farmer himself retires.

13 Following is an excerpt of the Lupoe family's suicide note.

"To start off about this tragic story, my name is Ervin Lupoe, my wife Ana Lupoe, my eldest daughter Brittney Lupoe-8yrs, my twin daughters Jaszmin, Jassely-5yrs, my twin boys Benjamin, Christian 2yrs 4mo. ….

My wife felt it better to end our lives and why leave our children in someone's else's hands, in addition, it seems Kiaser Permanente [previous employer] *wants us to kill ourselves and take our family with us. They did nothing to the manager who stated such, and did not attempt to assist us in the matter, knowing we have no job and 5 children under 8 years and with no place to go* [but the street]. *So here we are.*

Ervin Lupoe

Oh Lord my God is there no hope for a widow's son!"

14 Classical Analysis and Simulation of the Fractional Reserve System.

The simulation that follows models three banks. The First Bank has 200,000 depositors, and the Second and Third banks each have 100,000 depositors. For this simulation we use a *reserve requirement* of only 1 percent; this will generate a one hundred times (100X) *money multiplier effect.*

The first bank borrows $20 million to satisfy borrowing demands for its 200,000 customers. The Second and Third banks each borrow $10 million to support the borrowing demands of their 100,000 customers.

Following are tables A, B, and C. Table A represents the simulation that models the $20 million loaned to the First Bank. Table B represents the simulation that models the $10 million loaned to the Second Bank.

Note that tables A, B, and C are only excerpts of much larger tables. The simulations ran for one thousand iterations. That requires one thousand rows for each of the three simulation tables. Bank transactions were chosen randomly using a row of random number generators.

Random numbers were set to favor the First Bank over the other two banks by a factor of two to one. If the random number of a particular row was less than 0.5, then that row represents the First Bank. If the number was more than 0.5, but less than .75, then that row represents the Second bank, and if more than .75, then it represents the Third Bank. If anyone wishes to see the source file for this simulation they may contact debt. crisis@outlook.com

Table A 20,000,000	FIRST assets	BANK reserves	SECOND assets	BANK reserves	THIRD assets	BANK reserves
1	19,800,000	200,000	-	-	-	-
2	-	-	-	-	19,602,000	198,000
3	19,405,980	196,020	-	-	-	-
4	-	-	-	-	19,211,920	194,060
5	-	-	-	-	19,019,801	192,119
6	18,829,603	190,198	-	-	-	-
7	18,641,307	188,296	-	-	-	-
8	-	-	-	-	18,454,894	186,413

Table B 10,000,000	FIRST assets	BANK reserves	SECOND assets	BANK reserves	THIRD assets	BANK reserves
1	-	-	9,900,000	100,000	-	-
2	-	-	-	-	9,801,000	99,000
3	9,702,990	98,010	-	-	-	-
4	9,605,960	97,030	-	-	-	-
5	-	-	-	-	9,509,900	96,060
6	9,414,801	95,099	-	-	-	-
7	9,320,653	94,148	-	-	-	-
8	-	-	-	-	9,227,447	93,207

Table C 10,000,000	FIRST BANK assets	BANK reserves	SECOND BANK assets	BANK reserves	THIRD BANK assets	BANK reserves
1	-	-	-	-	9,900,000	100,000
2	9,801,000	99,000	-	-	-	-
3	9,702,990	98,010	-	-	-	-
4	-	-	9,605,960	97,030	-	-
5	9,509,900	96,060	-	-	-	-
6	-	-	9,414,801	95,099	-	-
7	9,320,653	94,148	-	-	-	-
8	-	-	9,227,447	93,207	-	-

Table 2 below shows the final results after combining all three simulations to make one complete simulation.

Table 2 Three sims combined	FIRST BANK assets	BANK reserves	SECOND BANK assets	BANK reserves	THIRD BANK assets	BANK reserves
	06,742,473	20,270,126	9,107,268	9,687,952	93,979,301	10,040,195

The First Bank borrowed $20 million and now has $2 billion of assets—for a one hundred times (100X) *money multiplier effect,* as expected with a reserve requirement of only 1%. The Second Bank borrowed $10 million and now has $1 billion of assets, and the same for Third Bank.

Of particular interest is the ratio of reserves to assets, they remain constant at 1 percent for all three banks. If the reserve requirement had been 5 percent, then this would give rise to a twenty-times (20X) *money multiplier effect* and so on.

Open Book Editions
A Berrett-Koehler Partner

Open Book Editions is a joint venture between Berrett-Koehler Publishers and Author Solutions, the market leader in self-publishing. There are many more aspiring authors who share Berrett-Koehler's mission than we can sustainably publish. To serve these authors, Open Book Editions offers a comprehensive self-publishing opportunity.

A Shared Mission

Open Book Editions welcomes authors who share the Berrett-Koehler mission—Creating a World That Works for All. We believe that to truly create a better world, action is needed at all levels—individual, organizational, and societal. At the individual level, our publications help people align their lives with their values and with their aspirations for a better world. At the organizational level, we promote progressive leadership and management practices, socially responsible approaches to business, and humane and effective organizations. At the societal level, we publish content that advances social and economic justice, shared prosperity, sustainability, and new solutions to national and global issues.

Open Book Editions represents a new way to further the BK mission and expand our community. We look forward to helping more authors challenge conventional thinking, introduce new ideas, and foster positive change.

For more information, see the Open Book Editions website:
http://www.iuniverse.com/Packages/OpenBookEditions.aspx

Join the BK Community! See exclusive author videos, join discussion groups, find out about upcoming events, read author blogs, and much more! http://bkcommunity.com/

www.ingramcontent.com/pod-product-compliance
Lightning Source LLC
Chambersburg PA
CBHW030935180526
45163CB00002B/574